Library of
Davidson College

NAPOLEON'S SOLDIERS IN AMERICA

NAPOLEON'S SOLDIERS IN AMERICA

By

Simone de la Souchère Deléry

PELICAN PUBLISHING COMPANY
GRETNA 1972

Copyright © 1950
By Le Cercle du Livre de France, Ltée.
Copyright © 1972
By Simone de la Souchère Deléry
All rights reserved under International
and Pan American Copyright Conventions
LCN: 74-186543
ISBN: 0-911116-58-3
First printing

Manufactured in the United States of America by
TJM Corporation, Baton Rouge, Louisiana

Book design by Oscar Richard
Jacket design by Gerald Bower

Published by Pelican Publishing Company, Inc.
630 Burmaster Street, Gretna, Louisiana 70053

Foreword

"Soldat de Napoléon I."

This brief but intriguing inscription, carved on a weather-worn tombstone in a little cemetery in south Louisiana, provided the catalyst for this significant historical work. A Napoleonic scholar of the first rank, the author discovered the inscription by chance many years ago and immediately launched a diligent quest for the long-forgotten trail of other Napoleonic exiles in America.

That her search was singularly successful is apparent. While her investigations carried her to the usual sources of historical research, the most productive explorations, perhaps, were her visits to innumerable descendants of these exiles. In back rooms and musty attics she found rusting family heirlooms and tattered documents which, when pieced together, added a new dimension to this exciting tale.

Early 19th century Europe had become a spawning ground for future Americans. Emigrants of virtually every nationality bargained, pleaded and indentured themselves in order to gain passage to opportunity in the New World. The Napoleonic Wars that had ravaged the continent had ended; the Emperor had been exiled to St.

Helena and his once-mighty *Grande Armée* lay in disarray. His devoted officers and soldiers harbored smoldering resentment toward the new Bourbon regime and dreamed of new and faraway lands. To many of them, the New World beckoned invitingly. After all, thousands of Frenchmen before them had found refuge in the United States, and, besides, hadn't Louisiana once belonged to France?

Some of the *demi-soldes* chose to make a new start in Pennsylvania, Texas or Alabama. The largest number, however, cast their fortunes with Louisiana, particularly the bustling port city of New Orleans.

One such individual was Pierre Benjamin Buisson, a veteran lieutenant of Napoleon's 6th Artillery, who arrived in the Queen City of the Mississippi River at the age of 24. He immediately found New Orleans to his liking. It was, in fact, not a great deal different from the France he once had known. The large Creole population was enthusiastically, almost fanatically, Bonapartist; the French language was preferred above all others; French customs were faithfully observed; and one could be recognized as a good citizen without giving up French citizenship. Furthermore, one could pledge undying allegiance to the prisoner of St. Helena while remaining loyal to one's newly adopted country.

Buisson and his former comrades in arms offered as much to America as they hoped to receive. They brought with them specific skills that proved to be invaluable to a young and growing nation. Among their number were many of the genuine nation-builders of 19th century America, men of education and daring who provided the skills as engineers, architects, city planners, physicians and writers that the emerging new nation required.

Even today, more than a century and a half later,

Foreword

Louisiana bears testimony to the influence of these military exiles—in the many street names that exalt Napoleon's victories; in the many hamlets and towns named after his various military campaigns; in the Code Napoleon, on which 20th century Louisiana Civil Code justice remains based; and in a French-speaking culture that, despite extensive Americanization, still endures.

Many important historical figures passed through New Orleans during the period covered by this book: an aging, but still proud Marquis de Lafayette, who came to this most French of American cities to enjoy for one last time a hero's acclaim; the bold, adverturesome Andrew Jackson, hero of the Battle of New Orleans, to whose side the Napoleonic exiles unselfishly rallied; and Dr. Francisco Antommarchi, the physician who ministered to a dying Napoleon at St. Helena.

The story of these Americanized Bonapartists is in large measure the history of exported French civilization in the 19th century. In tracing the lives of these former soldiers, the author provides a graphic account of the culture, customs, people and politics of early America.

This narrative biography fills a longstanding void in recorded American history and places in proper perspective the enduring Napoleonic—and French—influence in the development of these United States.

JAMES DOMENGEAUX
President
Council for the Development
of French in Louisiana
April 9, 1972

Acknowledgments

I SHOULD LIKE TO EXPRESS my gratitude to a great many individuals who provided me with invaluable assistance in the preparation of this work. I particularly want to acknowledge the efforts of the late Dean Roger McCutcheon, chairman of the Tulane University Council on Research; Dr. Garland Taylor, who headed the Howard-Tilton Library of Tulane University and is now Dean at Mercer University in Macon, Georgia; and Dr. Taylor's splendid staff, especially Miss Marguerite D. Renshaw.

Providing family papers or fruitful leads were the following New Orleans residents: Judge Henry Arnoult; the late Roger Baudier, editor of *Catholic Action of the South*; James F. Bezou; Fred N. Billingsley; James Buisson; Evans Casso; Wm. R. Cullison; Mrs. J. B. Donnes; Miss Emilie Doussan; Paul Louis Dupas, formerly librarian at Jackson Barracks; the late William Formento; the late James J. A. Fortier, curator of the Cabildo Museum; Mrs. Connie G. Griffith, head of the Special Collection of the Tulane University Library; Mrs. Edgar Hull; the late Mrs. Marie Generelly Lafargue; Mrs. Dagmar R. Lebreton; Mrs. Robert P. Linfield; George Perdreauville; Miss Margaret Ruckert, former head of the Louisiana

Department of the New Orleans Library; Dumond St. Martin; Edward Seghers, former director of the City Archives, Library of New Orleans; Sidney L. Villere; Rudolph H. Waldo, former custodian of the Notarial Archives of Orleans Parish; Samuel Wilson, Jr.; and André V. Wogan.

I am also indebted to the following individuals from other parts of Louisiana: the late Dr. Virgil Bedsole, former head of the Archives of the Louisiana State University Library at Baton Rouge; Marcel Bienvenu, editor of the *Teche News*, St. Martinville; Judge Kenneth Boagni, Opelousas; Mr. Ralph Buisson, Matthews; A. Charlet, Belle Alliance; Miss Lucille M. Cherbonnier, Gretna; Mrs. Grundy Cooper, Pineville; Miss Tommie Davis, Carville; Mrs. Thelma Dumez Duplantis, Chauvin; Mrs. Mary Alice Fontenot, Opelousas; Mrs. Ruth Fontenot, Opelousas; Ernest Gueymard, Baton Rouge; Mrs. Roy Krewitz, Breaux Bridge; Mrs. A. E. Neff, Covington; John Thistlewaite, editor of the *Opelousas Daily World*; Mrs. Dreux Vidrine, Ville Platte; Mrs. Alphonsine Charlet Wilbert, Donaldsonville; Henry W. Brandon; Mrs. T. L. Trawick; and the Misses Wartelle, Moundville.

From France, the following are due special thanks: General Bonnet de la Tour, Paris; Dr. Pierre Boye, Toulon; General Brissac, Paris; Dr. L. Guillot, Alençon; and Miss Marie Therese Pierront of the staff of the *Bibliothèque Nationale*, Paris.

Very special thanks go to Pierre Tisseyre, Director of the *Cercle du Livre de France*, Montreal, Canada for his cooperation in making the English edition of *A la Poursuite des Aigles* possible; to Jean Michel Pettinelli, French cultural attache in New Orleans, for his constant encouragement; and to Mrs. Andrée de Chateauneuf Heller for her patient help in typing the manuscript.

Contents

	Foreword	v
	Acknowledgments	ix
	Introduction	xv
I	Christmas Eve, 1817	3
II	White Cockade and Tricolor Flags	16
III	First Ties with the City	40
IV	The Tremoulet Hotel	51
V	Turmoil and Fever	69
VI	Death Comes to the Emperor	82
VII	Taps and Gun Salutes	95
VIII	Call from the Good Earth	108
IX	Printing and Planning	125
X	Dr. Antommarchi and Prince Murat	140
XI	The Napoleonic Legend in Louisiana Poetry	158
XII	Their Last War	174
XIII	The Elusive Séraphine	192
	Bibliography	199
	Index	207

Illustrations

Following page 78
    Lieutenant Pierre Benjamin Buisson
    Napoleon's Death Mask
    Dr. Francesco Antommarchi, Napoleon's Physician
    The Calaboose, Old Spanish Prison
    View From Roof of Tremoulet Hotel
    Map of Napoleon Avenue in 1835
    St. Helena Certificate

Following page 118
    St. Helena Medal
    General Charles Lallemand
    General Jean Joseph Amable Humbert
    Tombstone at Church of the Assumption
    Tomb of Garrigues de Flaugeac
    Napoleon House in New Orleans
    New Orleans Custom House in 1836
    Water Color by Fleury Generelly

Introduction

IT WAS QUITE BY ACCIDENT that I discovered the first of my Napoleonic exiles. We were riding along a blinding white road on a burning July afternoon. A brick church appeared, red as a flame in the intense blue sky. A French sign on the façade indicated it was the Eglise de l'Assomption. Its churchyard was enclosed by a rusty fence. According to my custom, I expressed a desire to visit it, tempted by those names often found in Louisiana: names of old French families or exotic first names which seem to spring from the pages of an 18th century novel: Delphine, Eulalie, Rose-Ange.

Suddenly, in the shadow of the church, on a well-kept tomb, I saw an inscription in huge letters: Pierre Charlet, *Soldat de Napoléon I*. For quite a while, I remained looking at those words, wondering who the man was who, after many years in America, had expressed the wish respected by his children to be forever identified by this title: Soldier of Napoleon I.

It took another hour of traveling before we finally discovered the home of Pierre Charlet's great-grandson. "He lives at Belle Alliance," a passerby had said. The name itself had a Napoleonic flavor. Belle Alliance was the farm where the Emperor spent a few hours before the fateful Waterloo battle. In Louisiana it recalled the uniting of two estates rather than a sad chapter of French history.

We arrived at the isolated home. On a wooden veranda three generations were taking their siesta on three rocking chairs. When the object of our visit was explained there was a happy surprise. A voice called out: "Adele, look on the top of the big armoire. You will find souvenirs from *Pépère's* father (*pépère* being the familiar appellation for grandfather)." The young girl came back, her arms loaded with objects which brought to my mind what has been called the legend of the eagles.

There were epaulettes with their fringe of tarnished gold, shoulder straps and a bayonet that Charlet probably had brought home as a trophy. Being an officer, he had a long pistol which had lain for so many years in its box lined with purple velvet and still bore a Belgian army manufacturer's address. There was the St. Helena medal, that medal which often was to be for me a valuable clue. "To my companion in glory my last thought," was engraved on it under Napoleon's profile.

How often I described this medal, telling people: "If you have one, it means that one of your ancestors has served in the First Empire's army." The discovery of Pierre Charlet launched me into the pursuit of his comrades, as I surmised that one seldom leaves his country alone if a national disaster has prompted his exile.

Wave after wave of French people had arrived on Louisiana shores: bold Norman sailors, Canadian *coureurs des bois*, aristocratic cadets bringing titles and empty purses, casket girls carrying their meager trousseau, Acadians driven from Nova Scotia by the English, *emigrés* from Revolutionary France, San Domingo planters fearing their rioting slaves. Each group has attracted the

Introduction xvii

attention of historians, novelists and poets. Why have the Bonapartist exiles remained in obscurity?

I tried to bring them to life. One by one, they began taking name and personality, thanks to the tomb inscriptions, diplomas, military service records, marching orders, letters, sketches and objects piously kept by their descendants.

People were most cooperative. A small town's newspaper would print on its first page: "If your great-grandfather has served Napoleon I, contact . . ." A radio would broadcast: "A visitor is interested in knowing if you have any mementoes of the First Empire Army . . ." Answers were coming. Then I had to sort them. The desire to find the right ancestor might influence some, while other timid souls had to be encouraged.

"I have two large bags full of French papers. They are in the attic. It is mighty hot up there!"

"Allow me to come at six in the morning, before the sun strikes the roof."

Or: "Cousin Odile knows more than I do about the past."

"Where does Cousin Odile live?"

When names or dates were not accompanied by documents, I made it a point to search court archives or church registers. Another helpful source was the press, so unbelievably active in Louisiana during the first half of the 19th century. Old gazettes, as the newspapers were called, showed me my exiles (as I had come to call them) looking for work, expressing political opinions, becoming entangled in local controversies, receiving praise or blame and even writing songs and poems.

How were they received in their new country? How did they react to climate and inhabitants? What contribution did they make? Occasionally I took the liberty of guessing some of their feelings. This, however, was not arbitrary. Conditions that made sarcastic Northerners say: "See New Orleans and die" (meaning that fevers, floods, and fires were always ready to strike), luckily do not exist anymore. Residents take in stride the long hot summers, the short winters squeezed between a springlike autumn and a dazzling spring. Some characteristics have remained: the Louisianians' hospitality, their *joie de vivre*, and their love of feasts and parades that they may have inherited from one of their governors, the Grand Marquis Rigaud de Vaudreuil who held court on Royal Street. Therefore, a French citizen's reactions when landing in 1817 may not have been very different from the ones experienced by a 20th century European. Moreover, anecdotes related through generations provide an insight into the thought of yesteryear.

These exiles, proud of having fought under the gold eagles of Napoleon's flags, proud of their records bearing an eagle seal, deserve to be known. As some of the turbulent eddies which form our Mississippi River, they contributed their share to the heritage France bequeathed to Louisiana.

NAPOLEON'S SOLDIERS IN AMERICA

I

Christmas Eve, 1817

IT WAS CHRISTMAS EVE, 1817. It was a Christmas eve that resembled a spring evening with its deep, velvety, dark blue sky and fantastic shadows projected from wrought iron balconies on narrow, dry mud streets. Here and there, from a *porte-cochère*, escorted ladies came out, all soft voices, light laughs, and silk dresses under lacy shawls. Out of half-open tavern doors boisterous songs burst forth.

There was nothing religious in the atmosphere, yet, the church was not far away. St. Louis Cathedral, with its two bell-shaped steeples, stood dedicated to the most saintly of the kings of France (or rather to the only saint among them), Louis IX, the Crusader. It was flanked by two buildings, regular, sturdy, having the quiet dignity of city halls. Pale yellow in the moonlight, the structures faced an almost deserted fenced square. Rows of two-story houses above tightly shuttered little shops ringed the square. A traveler from France might have recalled in the Place d'Armes the main square of almost any provincial town of his own country.

Such a traveler was there. Wrapped in the mildness of that December night, hearing a woman's voice singing a lullaby from which French words emerged with slurring sounds, he wondered what New Orleans was most surprising for—its familiarity or its remoteness.

That very morning he had landed after two long months on the ocean and two wearisome days sailing slowly up through the greyish delta. The vigorous beating of the waves on the hull of the boat had been replaced by the almost inaudible flapping against a shore so sunken that it scarcely resembled the edge of a new continent. At night *L'Amérique* stopped. Clouds of mosquitoes surged up from the willows. Passengers remained on deck, less disturbed by the bites and buzzing than by emotions stirred for some by homecoming, for others by discovery. At dawn the vessel started again. The swampy banks were becoming firmer. Bushes appeared, then a few orange trees, identifiable by their pale gold fruit. Children running along the river edge shouted to the voyagers. "They sound French," travelers said smiling. Ahead rose an embankment, the sole protection of the harbor from the mighty Mississippi.

The voyage's monotony had been broken only by a pirate's threat in the Gulf of Mexico. At this moment, one young man had almost wished for a chance to fight. More than two months of quiet and idleness were almost more than he could bear. This same traveler wondered in the softness of that December night whether the new world would ever bring back to him the turbulent life he had cherished. He looked at the stars, remembering a trip from Paris to Metz six years earlier. He had climbed to the top seat of the stagecoach and through that April night in Lorraine, colder than this December night in Louisiana, he had gazed at the stars. Above New Orleans they seemed larger, brighter, and the exile felt somewhat comforted.

Once ashore, he began to wander about the city, but

even when wandering he walked at a brisker pace than the other pedestrians. Some of them turned to look at him, with his tightly buttoned long redingote flapping on his boots. As he turned a corner, a delicious aroma of hot bread brought a flood of memories. A baker was standing on his threshold, shoulders shining with sweat, face white with flour, so much like any French baker that the stranger could not resist calling out to him: "Working on Christmas eve?"

"Yes, for Père Antoine's protégés."

"Père Antoine?"

"You don't know him? You must have just landed. A Frenchman from France, of course!"

The Frenchman from France smiled. How often he would hear this expression in the future; it would always be associated with the odor of Cadet Molon's hot oven.

A wider street ran behind the Cathedral. A half-burned hall opened its blackened gaping mouth. A poster called for workers to help rebuild Mr. Davis' theater. As payment they would receive shares in the undertaking. Here was something to do, but how would shares in a future theater take care of present needs?

Along a small garden behind the Cathedral, his head covered with a hood and dragging his sandals, a monk was walking, followed by two altar boys. It was almost midnight but only a few persons were entering the church. From a long building music wafted through the night air. A voice whispered: "Would you like to go to the Octoroons' ball?"

"The Octoroons?"

"Yes, *Monsieur*, a little *café au lait* but charming!"

"I don't know how to dance."

The man who had refused the invitation raised his head and looked at the second floor windows. The light falling from a lamp-post revealed his firm features, blue-grey eyes and slightly curly brown hair beneath his tilted-back hat. Standing still, he observed the ballroom: olive-skinned women, with bright flowers in their jet black hair, dancing with elegantly dressed white gentlemen. How young they all looked compared to the stranger who had been aged by several years of hard studies and still harder fights. He did not know whether he envied them or felt contempt. He was more lonely than ever. Would he go back to his cousins' home?

Earlier the same day he had been welcomed by Mr. Guillotte. Curious young faces leaned over the banister of the tall staircase. "Sophie, Elizabeth, Marie Pétronille, Pierre, come to greet your cousin!" The boy had shaken his hand according to the new style. The girls with eyes lowered had made a short curtsy.

The stranger stopped a moment to determine the way to Guillotte's house. On a gate, an escutcheon bearing a *fleur de lys* attracted his attention. The words *Consulat de France* could be read in the semi-darkness. A furrow seemed to cut the plaque in two. He touched the marble. The *fleur de lys* was cracked. The word *France* had brought back the lurking nostalgia. No, he would not go back to his cousins now, for they were already part of this foreign land. He would look for exiles such as himself who could understand him. He remembered an address given to him and asked directions to the *Le Veau Qui Tète* (The Suckling Calf). "No luck, Sir," he was told. "Bruno Ravel is moving to a new location and his inn is closed tonight, but on Levee Street several cafés are still open at this hour."

A breeze blew in from the river and he walked toward it. The levee appeared as a long bulky embank-

Christmas Eve, 1817

ment on the other side of which ghost-like masts and sails seemed to spring from nowhere. There were the wooden steps he had climbed down for his first contact with American soil. Nearby was a market which that morning swarmed with motions, sounds, colors, smells: the red and yellow of *tignons* wrapped around the heads of Negro women, the indigo of cotton skirts, the rainbow-like feathers and beads of Indians offering fragrant herbs from woven baskets and the silvery glitter of fish on trays. Tall white-skinned longshoremen called to each other in guttural voices, drowning the softer singing tones of people of all colors watching the passengers land. Now, as night subdued the activity, only the sickening smell of wilted vegetables and overipe fruit lingered. Facing the levee were a few lights shining on café signs. Frenchmen would be there, less bent on drinking than on talking.

The stranger walked slowly to the café and peered through the cloudy panes of glass. Inside, at each table, a candle lighted hands holding cards or throwing dice, long aristocratic fingers or short paws with dirty nails. Unfamiliar accents drifted outside. Suddenly, the man stopped short. Through a half-open door he could see silent, motionless men. Opposite them, on the wall, a silhouette appeared: a profile, topped by a large hat, with sharp features in spite of a double chin, an epaulette, an arm bent over the chest, the hand having disappeared between two buttons of the uniform.

"Am I dreaming?" the stranger wondered. As if in a trance, he entered the room. He saw that the shadow on the wall was being projected by the carved knob of a cane a man held in front of a candle. For two years these canes had been familiar objects in the hands of Napoleon's former soldiers. How many conversations were held, how many plans discussed in front of the phantom they conjured? Who were those men who, in a New Orleans café, mute with respect, gazed at the Imperial image?

The men soon became aware of the new spectator. There was a whisper, a muffled curse. Chairs were pushed away, a blow from the back of a hand snuffed out the light. The newcomer stepped forward. Erect, standing at attention, a hand to his temple, he saluted and introduced himself: "Lieutenant Pierre Benjamin Buisson of the 6th Artillery Regiment of the *Grande Armée*."

In the darkness hoarse voices answered, *"Vive l'Empereur!"*

Ex-Lieutenant Pierre Benjamin Buisson was born at the most tragic moment of the French Revolution, in the spring of 1793. The King had just been beheaded, political parties were sending each other to the guillotine, heavy tumbrels were rumbling on the Paris pavements bringing priests, aristocrats, and other "suspects" to their deaths while Europe in arms was trying to break through the frontiers.

It was Benjamin Buisson's maternal grandfather, Alexandre Guillotte, whose address had a revolutionary flavor—Section des Sans-culottes—who signed the birth certificate, the father being away in the army in the *"service de la patrie."* There could not have been much rejoicing in the little home on the street of the Five Diamonds. Who knew when and where a priest could be found to baptize the newly born child of Jean François Claude Buisson and Marie Esther Guillotte?

The foreign invasion having been checked, the father returned to resume his career as a merchant and laboriously raise his sons, Pierre Benjamin and Frederic. Meanwhile in France a new power was growing that was soon to claim for its service every father and every son.

Pierre Benjamin was eleven when Napoleon Bonaparte became Emperor. As did all Parisians, he must have cheered the cortege going to Notre Dame for the coronation. As most boys of that time, he must have listened to endless stories told by the *grognards,* the Emperor's devotees, who grumbled but always followed him.

How eager Pierre Benjamin was to see the day come when he could take part in the marvelous adventure. His parents, aware of his clear thinking, power of reasoning and love for figures and problems, suggested that their son try to enter the newly organized Ecole Polytechnique. This "School of Public Works," as it was first called, was the outcome of the Commission of *Travaux Publics* created by Carnot, the "Organizer of Victory" during the darkest hours of the Revolutionary wars. He had shown more insight than most of his colleagues in the Convention that had sent the chemist Lavoisier to the guillotine with the terse statement: "The Republic does not need scientists."

The Directoire, next in power, decided that new schools should embody the trend toward scientific and practical knowledge as the French Encyclopedists had urged. The Ecole Polytechnique was to rank at the top of the system. As soon as he became First Consul, Bonaparte encouraged its development. As Emperor, he drew from it his best officers. He spoke of it as "the first school of the world," the "envy of Europe," the "hen that lays for me golden eggs."

One of these golden eggs became young Buisson when, after taking the difficult entrance examination, he received a letter from the school's governor advising him he had been admitted with the number 48.

That was in September of 1811. Napoleon felt that

he owned the world, a world he would bequeath to his newly born son, the King of Rome. Dapper in his blue uniform with scarlet lapels, Pierre Benjamin also felt on top of the world. But his career on St. Genevieve Mount in the Latin Quarter did not run smoothly. To be eighteen, to be a part of the intellectual elite of a country where a spirit of criticism is always rampant, and to be submitted to the harshest discipline was not easy. One autumn day Buisson's parents, at home at their new address on Cloître St. Méry Street, received a letter announcing that their son, having taken part in a "mutiny," had been expelled from Polytechnique.

For his punishment the cadet was sent to Rennes as a simple private. This exile in the Breton capital did not last long, however, since in the spring of 1813, after having been reinstated, he graduated with his class. A choice then had to be made. A civilian career, of course, was unthinkable at that time. What kind of regiment would young Pierre Benjamin like to join? The *Grande Armée* had just straggled back from Russia, its 400,000 men reduced to less than 80,000. The Emperor was depending more and more on his artillery. Buisson was sent to Metz's Ecole d'Application where in the old fortified Lorraine city he would receive his practical training as an artillery officer.

It was customary to remain there for two years but time was pressing. The war was coming nearer. More and more Napoleon needed his "golden eggs." Six months after he entered Metz's school, Second Lieutenant Buisson was ordered to report to Mayence and ask *Monsieur le Colonel* where to join his regiment. This was the moment he had been waiting for, but instead of the splendid cavalcade across conquered kingdoms, it was going to be a bloody struggle for each foot of French soil.

Christmas Eve, 1817

Outnumbered five to one by European enemies and trying to protect Paris, Napoleon threw his armies against Blücher and Schwartzenberg from the River Marne to the River Oise, from the Yonne to the Seine. On the chalky roads of Champagne, on the golden slopes of Burgundy, in the curves of the Ile de France, north, south, west, east, back and forth, inch by inch, Second Lieutenant Buisson fought. From February 1 to March 26 he took part in eleven battles: La Rothière, three times at Nogent, and Nangis, and Montereau where his horse was killed under him, and Troyes, and Bar sur Aube, and Pont de la Guillotine at the gates of Troyes, and Troyes again where he lost all his baggage, and Vitry; then in haste to St. Dizier to cut the Austrians' and Prussians' communication with the rear. The Allies showed little concern. Intercepted messages had revealed that Paris was rising against Napoleon. They kept on marching toward Paris. Buisson remained at St. Dizier and was spared the sight of the enemies parading in front of the newly erected *Arc de Triomphe.*

A story went around which was not recorded in official documents but handed down to other generations. At Montereau, after a bullet hit his horse, Buisson rolled in the mud and dashed toward his battery. A higher ranking officer rushed to him, shouting: "Too late, cease fire!" Rebellious, Pierre Benjamin turned to his men: "Fire!" A second messenger came, then a third: "Order from the Emperor, cease fire!" Buisson's battery still fired.

That night, Napoleon rode through the battlefield with his faithful companion General Lefebvre-Desnouettes. He stopped in front of the exhausted lieutenant, spoke briefly with an officer, and, staring at the petrified young man, said, "Had you not understood the order? One of my stubborn Polytechnicien, very likely.

You should be punished, Captain." Then, with a smile which belied the words, he pinned his own cross of the Legion of Honor on Buisson's tunic.

Six weeks after the Montereau incident two diplomas reached Pierre Benjamin. One appointed him, not captain, but first lieutenant; the second awarded him the Legion of Honor. What magnificent presents these would have been for the young man's twenty-first birthday! Unfortunately, the date was April 2, 1814. Paris had fallen.

While Napoleon was in exile at Elba, Buisson and thousands of his comrades were dismissed from the army and alloted only half pay (*demi-solde*) by Louis XVIII. Upon the Emperor's return, Buisson rushed to his service again. He was not at Waterloo on the fatal day, but while at Lille awaiting orders he saw the haggard remnants of the *Grande Armée* straying through the Flanders fields.

For a brief interval, rather than to share the *demi-soldes'* endless reminiscing at the Café Lambertin, which was redolent with brandy, he accepted a reinstatement offered by the Bourbon regime. He was attached to the La Fère regiment and garrisoned at Auxonne. That was the very location where more than twenty-five years before an obscure Corsican—one Napoleon Bonaparte— had started his prestigious career. To serve in the Royal Army there seemed even more of a betrayal; Pierre Benjamin resigned his commission.

What could civilian life offer him? What could France, bled to death by an army of occupation, do to relieve the plight of thousands of ex-soldiers? Adding to the general misery, crops in the season following Waterloo were very poor. How could Frenchmen remain optimistic while munching a grayish, chalky bread?

It was known that the Emperor's brother Joseph,

former King of Spain, already had settled in Philadelphia. High-ranking officers had joined him, some of them chased out of Europe by the Bourbons' police. But what about men with little or no financial resources?

Europe exiles us
Happy children of the forests
Hear our sad story
Savages, we are French
Have pity on our glory!

This song and another one with the refrain, "Laurels grow in Champ d'Asile," were heard all over Paris. The words had been written by Pierre Jean de Béranger, whose popularity was rising, and printed in the *Minerve Française*, a newspaper published by the liberal Benjamin Constant. The *Minerve* did more than focus attention on Napoleonic veterans through poems and articles; it began collecting funds to send them to America.

People responded, some out of kindness and some out of a spirit of opposition to the regime, unaware that this regime was delighted to rid itself of troublesome *demi-soldes*. There was also among the best-read Frenchmen an element of curiosity. What an opportunity to find whether wild nature was as compassionate to men as Jean Jacques Rousseau had stated!

Why, for example, were Paul and Virginie, depicted in Bernardin de St. Pierre's novel, innocent and happy as long as they remained on a far-away island? Why did Manon Lescaut, the wretched heroine of Abbé Prevost's story, find redemption in a Louisiana desert? This theory of a return to nature and the magic of exotic countries appealed to a number of Parisians who, in the bottom of their hearts, had not the slightest desire to leave their beloved capital.

This plan also stirred the imagination of Bordeaux residents who could admire in their Public Park evergreen oaks and cypresses, their long snake-like roots twisted in enormous balls of Louisiana soil, which a fad had caused to be brought to France at the end of the 18th century.

Among the people strolling through that park were many *demi-soldes*, 300 of them having taken refuge in that port. The departure of a ship being almost a daily occurence, exile for them was easier to visualize.

The *Minerve Française*'s readers, well acquainted with Mr. de Chateaubriand's description of the Meschacebé,* could already imagine their protégés coming down the Father of Waters on a floating island among caribou and pistias. What caribou and pistias actually were remained somewhat obscure. Even the buffalo and bullfrogs appearing in *Atala* and *Les Natchez* seemed mythical creatures. How fortunate were the travelers invited to become acquainted with these mysterious fauna and flora! One repeated this in prose and in verse, the future emigrants repeating it louder than others, like someone whistling in the dark.

True to French traditions, councils must have been held in the Buisson home. It was obvious that the frustrated, somber young man was eager to leave Europe. Would he join one of the groups the *Minerve* was taking under its wings? "A Polytechnicien going to clip the underbrush and fell trees!" the father must have growled in dismay.

Names of places that already had attracted a few Frenchmen were tossed about: the banks of the St. Law-

---

* Name used by early French travelers referring to the Mississippi River.

Christmas Eve, 1817

rence River, Pennsylvania, Alabama. Few doubted that from the Hudson Bay to the Gulf of Mexico those good neighbors would extend a helping hand to each other, ready to lend hammer or salt. There had been an exile on the maternal side of the family, a former bodyguard of Louis XVI who had fled France during the Revolution. Practical and motherly Madame Buisson may have suggested: "Why would not Pierre Benjamin go to visit his cousins Guillotte? First, they had lived at Elizabethtown. Then they moved south to a port still French after 14 years of American rule—*la Nouvelle Orléans*."

Ex-Lieutenant Buisson tucked in his baggage two copies of his birth certificate, the letter admitting him to the Ecole Polytechnique, his *feuilles de route* or orders to report to various garrisons, his *états de service* stating ranks, campaigns, and distinctions, his Legion of Honor diploma and, of course, the beloved star-shaped cross itself. Then, in October 1817 he sailed on *L'Amérique* for New Orleans.

II

White Cockade and Tricolor Flags

"GET ACQUAINTED WITH OUR CITY and do not hesitate to ask questions," the obliging Mr. Guillotte had said.

Accepting the suggestion, Pierre Benjamin walked toward Bourbon Street. He had noticed a sign hanging above a door: *Cabinet de Lecture* (reading room). It was a place where he could perhaps read the latest news from Europe, news arriving through New York or Philadelphia and finding its place in local newspapers while he was still at sea.

He examined the pages of the *Gazette de la Louisiane,* the *Courrier de la Louisiane,* and the *Ami des Lois,* delighting in the discovery that at least two out of the four pages of each were printed in French. Nothing important had happened since his departure. Out of curiosity or idleness he looked at the announcements of lotteries; at the death notices where the name of the deceased was invariably followed by the words *honnête homme* (gentleman); and at the invitation to a meeting of a Freemason lodge. He read the offer of rewards for anyone who would bring back a *marron* slave, an adjective which puzzled him until he found its meaning (fugitive) conveyed by a pathetic vignette showing a Negro running away with his bundle of clothes. There were also offers and requests for work, a good thing for a newcomer to remember.

Then his eyes fell on the spectacle offered that very evening at the Théâtre d'Orléans, a drama on the theme of a prince who had lost his throne: "His misfortunes and the resemblances of his fate with the fate of the most illustrious of French exiles are deemed to attract spectators' curiosity and interest the sensitive souls to the plight of a man whose memory will leave deep traces in the hearts of his admirers and in posterity." So in this city, as in Paris, newspapers were stirring sympathy for the St. Helena prisoner.

"French people are not exiles here, my friend," he had been told by Guillotte "They are at home." Who would know better than the former royal bodyguard working as a horse dealer in Louisiana? Why had his young cousin referred to himself as an exile? Had not this harbor founded a century ago by a Canadian of Norman origin, Jean Baptiste de Bienville, and named in honor of the Regent, Duke of Orleans, remained French in spite of forty years under the Spanish regime and fourteen years as part of the United States?

Pierre Benjamin had to admit that everything he had seen or read since his arrival made him share Mr. Guillotte's opinion. That very morning coming out of the *cabinet de lecture* he had been accosted by two young men who, noticing his red ribbon of the *Légion d'Honneur,* had asked questions about his military career. "If we ever can be of service to you . . ." and they had introduced themselves: "Jacques and Enoul de Livaudais." The voices were slightly patronizing but friendly. "We are not French like you. We are Creoles."

What did they mean? Mr. Guillotte must have

furnished an explanation that other incidents would strengthen. Strictly speaking, a Creole was anyone born in the West Indies or Louisiana of French or Spanish parents. There even were purists who insisted that to receive this title (almost a title of nobility) one's parents should have settled in Louisiana before the Louisiana Purchase. It was the equivalent to having had a grandfather on the *Mayflower*. Many Creoles were the offspring of younger sons of noble families. The pre-Revolution French law granting the entire inheritance to the eldest son had deprived the cadets of any worldly goods. Many of them in the course of the 18th century sought adventure and fortune in the New World. It goes without saying that the Creoles were pure Caucasian. When the *Gazette* or the *Courrier* advertised the sale of a Creole slave, the readers knew it meant that the slave had not been imported from Africa, that he was as much a product of Louisiana as a head of lettuce also called creole. White of skin and blue-blooded were the Creoles.

Sons and grandsons of the *Chevaliers*, a title often given to the cadets, had the pleasant task of welcoming the aristocrats fleeing from the threat of the guillotine. Newcomers took out of their trunks silk dresses or lace cuffs worn at Versailles. Instead of the rough pioneers' life in a log cabin, they danced in Royal Street salons. Instead of carving a field out of forest, they strutted along streets named Toulouse, Maine, Conti, or Condé after princes. Some of the princes were illegitimate and the streets often were muddy. But, *qu'importe*, what was the difference? A remnant of the *Ancien Regime*'s elegant way of life still flourished in Louisiana.

Orleanians felt more at ease when they learned that the Isle d'Orléans, as this section was called, was going to be French again instead of Spanish. They prepared their homes to receive the First Consul's envoy with grandeur. In the place of the expected General Victor only his aide de camp showed up. But he was the young and handsome André Burthe d'Annelet, so Orleanians opened wide their salons to him and introduced their daughters.

The joy of becoming French again lasted but twenty days. Then the Prefect, Clement de Laussat, announced that his government had sold Louisiana to the United States. When the French flag came down in the Place d'Armes, there were tears in many eyes. "Thus Monsieur de Buonaparte has abandoned us," the *Moniteur* wrote in icy tones.

The Creoles did not resent this abandonment for long. No season was gayer than the winter of 1803–1804. When suppers and balls ended, no lanterns carried by slaves were needed to escort the masters home. Often, from the bank of the river where tall blond Kentuckians unloaded barges, the party watched the sunrise. Unpleasant incidents were rare. One evening dancers harshly ordered bewildered musicians to stop an American quadrille and play a French minuet. Sometimes, through half-open shutters, uneasy citizens pricked their ears to follow the clashing of dueling swords in the little garden behind the cathedral. But, nevertheless, dueling was an exciting pastime.

Buisson and other newcomers listening to the account of the events during the previous fifteen years must have been surprised by that rather easy acceptance of a foreign regime on the part of people so French at heart. Had Louisianians merely proceeded on faith alone? Was a document going to change their language and customs? Never, they thought. If one of these strangers, as they insisted on calling the Americans, wished to be received in their homes, he would need a letter of introduction from a well-qualified person, and naturally he would have to express himself in French.

Practical minds also thought that in case of danger more rapid help could come from Washington than from Paris. Who was the enemy? England, naturally. While changing flags one could preserve the same anti-British spirit. Perhaps Mr. de Buonaparte had been wise. Wise also he had been when he chose a Creole for his wife, feminine society said. "*A Tascher de la Pagerie, chère,* from Martinique!"

When later one heard that for the future of his dynasty Napoleon had married Marie-Louise of Austria, Creoles lamented Josephine's repudiation more loudly than Louisiana's abandonment. Often a duet was heard coming from the second-story salon of a tall residence. A soprano tearfully was answering a baritone: "Let us hope that the other will give you happiness but if you ever need me, Sire, I will come back, I will come back." "Josephine's adieux to Napoleon," passers-by whispered with reverence. "One never tires of this song here!"

Adding fuel to the Bonapartist fire were the San Domingo* refugees, both civilian and military. There was a strong link between Louisiana and West Indies Creoles. Frenchmen who in the 18th century sailed to the Caribbean islands did not foresee the disasters their descendants would have to meet. Excited by news of the Paris revolution and agitated by undercover British agents, slaves were revolting. Guadeloupe was easily pacified but Haiti presented fearful problems. When Bonaparte's expedition, wrecked by fevers, was unable to protect them, planters escaped horrible reprisals by moving

---

* The western part of the Island of Haiti was referred to in the 18th century as Saint Domingue by the French settlers, translated here as San Domingo.

to other islands. But when a French army brought war to Spain the Spanish residents of the West Indies drove out the French. As a result, Isle d'Orleans which according to the 1806 census had 17,000 inhabitants had, by 1809, increased its population by 6,000 refugees. One-third were white and the rest were free men of color, plus some slaves clinging to their masters either out of devotion or out of the fear of newly acquired freedom. As the importing of "ebony wood" had been forbidden in Louisiana since 1807, the Legislature passed a regulation allowing impoverished owners to keep their servants who could sometimes be leased to others.

It is a wonder that those miserable people so inadequately protected by the First Consul's army and who therefore had become the target of English bullets and Spanish insults did not hate Revolutionary and Imperial France. Yet, as did their Louisiana counterparts, the *Créoles des Isles,* they rejoiced at news of Napoleon's victories.

At the Café des Exilés Buisson must have met the first wave of military refugees: the remnant of the San Domingo expedition. A British fleet blocked the route to Europe. The defeated soldiers boarded any vessel. The Mississippi delta proved hospitable. Had they the right to remain? It would take nearly a year to explain their plight to their chiefs in France, to receive an order, and to report to another post across the ocean. It was easier to keep quiet and remain. They remained.

"Here there are about twenty adventurers from Bordeaux and San Domingo, well informed, confident of Bonaparte's invincibility and the French nation's power," wrote Louisiana Governor W. C. C. Claiborne, a Virginian. Would not those twenty, and many more who followed, bring a disquieting spirit?

Perhaps it was to counterbalance their influence that the Governor welcomed General Moreau. Buisson must have been stunned. "General Moreau?" "Yes, General Moreau who had been victorious at Hohenlinden." "But he became a traitor and Bonaparte banished him!"

Yet, Moreau was not unfavorably remembered in New Orleans. The son of a lawyer from Brittany, Jean Victor Marie Moreau was a law student when his comrades elected him head of a battalion of volunteers at the army's first call for help. Three years later he had risen to the rank of general when he received the news that his father had been put to death by a revolutionary tribunal. This was enough to make him hate everything connected with the new regime. He was also influenced by the example of two of his former commanders-in-chief, Dumouriez and Pichegru, who, each in turn, had betrayed the French government.

Welcomed by Bonaparte in Paris, introduced by Madame Bonaparte to a Creole, Mademoiselle Hulot, whom he later married, he nevertheless appeared as the center of opposition to the growing power of the First Consul. Placed in non-activity, he was compromised in the affair of the *machine infernale,* that devilish contraption which was intended to kill Bonaparte on his way to the Opera and missed him by a few minutes. Proved innocent but still under suspicion, Moreau was banished. Having sailed from Cadiz with his wife, he arrived in New Orleans and settled in the French Consul's residence.

It was almost the case of the escaped lion finding refuge in its own cage. This strange situation puzzled Governor Claiborne. Consul Desforges, while expressing fear that his government might not be satisfied, explained uneasily that he could not close his door upon an old friend. And so the General, polite, courteous and, above all, husband of a Creole, became a favorite in New Orleans society. But in 1813, when the news came that Moreau, now an advisor of the enemy, had been struck and killed by a French cannon ball on the Dresden battlefield, the loyal Bonapartists agreed the traitor had received his just due.

Newcomers must have wondered if everyone in the city was a Bonapartist. The answer came in an unexpected way.

"Your Napoleon! He is the Prince of Egotists! Turpin, another glass of gouave!" bellowed a giant with shaggy grey hair and shabby clothes.

Exclamations, some of anger and some of amusement, filled the air. Hearing his hero insulted, an ex-lieutenant such as Buisson must have rushed forward, his hand feeling for his sword in a hard-to-forget gesture. "Let us get out of here. You cannot fight with an older man, with a General. Had I known Humbert had come back from Mexico I would not have brought you here," Guillotte said.

No doubt Buisson then heard Jean Amable Humbert's story. It was a story told a hundred times by Humbert himself to all the Orleanians—or, rather, to the customers of Thiot's café on St. Philip Street or, further down, Turpin's cabaret, which faced the estate of bon vivant Bernard de Marigny who occasionally joined the motley, jolly, roistering crowd.

"Another glass of gouave for the General!" someone called out. The General no doubt had become acquainted with this fermented juice of the guava tree at San Domingo. The acquaintance had changed into a lasting familiarity which must have had its share in giving Humbert's weather-beaten face this ruddy color.

Whenever he was half-sober, all the events of his

past revived in his memory. He did not hide the fact that during his youth he had gone through Lorraine villages calling: *"Peaux d'lapins, marchand de peaux d'lapins!"* (Rabbit skins, peddler of rabbit skins!) Farmers' wives would deliver into his hands the malodorant bloody furs which he would resell at the nearest town.

One day, a sergeant looking for recruits persuaded the young giant to join the army. In a few strides he reached the top rank. In 1792 men were needed to fight the Royalists in Vendee and repulse the foreign coalition. Humbert, with his younger colleague, Hoche, did both. In Prussia, he led his men in scaling a plateau. Waving his sword above his head, he gave the command to charge: *"Chargez, mes enfants, Landau ou la mort!"* (Charge, my children, Landau or death!) After Landau was taken, Humbert and Hoche were sent to Ireland to strike the English from the rear. The plan failed, but their courage in the face of impossible odds was long remembered. Humbert later was wounded while commanding the army of the Danube. Then came the San Domingo adventure.

As he related the tale, Humbert lowered his voice and listeners huddled around him. Refugees from Pointe à Pitre or Cap François might smile hearing him describe how the gallant officers guided young beauties away from burning homes and ambushed Negroes. Actually it had not been so glamorous. The expeditionary corps had to fight the cruel Christophe and Dessalines and the wise Toussaint L'Ouverture, whose capture through betrayal and imprisonment caused embarrassment, if not remorse. Worst of all were the fevers, dysentery, and the *vomito negro* which distorted the bodies and soiled the uniforms.

Humbert also had occasion to serve Napoleon's sister. Pauline Bonaparte had not wished to sail to the West Indies, but her brother had ordered her to accompany her husband, Marshal Leclerc, selected to head the expedition. He was one of the many victims of yellow fever. His widow cut her hair as a sign of mourning which prompted the First Consul to remark: "Paulette must be sure that it will grow more beautiful!" Before her hair had had time to grow, Madame Leclerc had chosen Humbert as one of the officers who would escort her on the long trip home. She needed consolation and the herculean, resplendent general performed his new duty with his usual dash. At least, this is what Orleanians were led to believe.*

Bonaparte was grooming his family with an eye to the fast approaching Imperial status, and rumors of his favorite sister's conduct were not to his liking. Humbert felt he was being pushed away and vociferously expressed his resentment. "Who does this little Corsican think he is?" Humbert thundered. Toward which goal was he leading the Republic? Echoes of the stentorian voice reached the Emperor-to-be.

General Humbert received the order to go to Brittany. After the Haitian turmoil, inactivity under grey skies in sleepy towns was more than he could stand. He heard of a boat sailing for New Orleans. Without waiting for an official authorization, he sailed on it. For a while his rank, his uniform, his flamboyance, his tales of conquest brought him invitations in New Orleans. His brusque manners and coarse language, however, were not suitable in Creole salons. In the port he found more suitable companions without difficulty.

"Let him alone with his pirates!" Mr. Guillotte had warned his young cousin. Pierre Benjamin was not long in noticing that Orleanians of any rank, indeed even the

* In fact, Humbert's return preceded Pauline's.

Creoles, spoke of the pirates with amused leniency. They were always willing to offer this explanation to newcomers: "Jean Laffite and Dominique You are not pirates. They are privateers. They stop only the enemy's vessels." What enemy? Very conveniently in the Gulf of Mexico and on adjoining seas one could always find a country ready to place its official seal on a *lettre de marque* granting captains permission to board a ship belonging to a hostile nation. Around 1815 the tiny Republic of Carthagene revolted against Spain and became a convenient source of *lettres de marque*.

Reading the correspondence between the plenipotentiary minister in Washington, Serurier, and his subordinate in New Orleans, Tousac,* one can surmise that the French consul had been solicited to show the same broad-mindedness as Carthagene. But Washington was adamant: Only His Majesty the Emperor, Monsieur, could grant *lettres de marque*.

About the same time, Tousac was officially warned "not to enter in any of General Humbert's plans. . . . You could have suspected that he would be on the banks of the Elbe and not in New Orleans if he were beyond reproach. . . . Moreover, it will not take you long to perceive the disorder of his poor head . . . in spite of his pretension to be a leader he will only damage the side he will choose." So wrote Serurier in November, 1813.

French officials were much more severe than the Orleanians. To the latter, Humbert was what the Spaniards would have called *simpatico*. And so was one of his best friends, Jean Laffite.

"You should meet Laffite," newly arrived men often were told, especially if they were ex-soldiers. It was ru-

* Often referred to as Touzac, he signed his letters Tousac.

White Cockade and Tricolor Flags 27

mored that the dark, elegant Bordelais had once been one of Bonaparte's lieutenants. Laffite let this fact be known when, temporarily, he opened a fencing school. Otherwise, he dropped a veil of mystery on his past as a true buccaneer of the romantic era should. About the present, everyone knew that he reigned over the delta, the Gulf, and their myriad of islets and bayous, the latter being the name for narrow and slow streams as numerous as the capillary vessels of the body. Laffite was powerful and bold enough to hold the Governor in check. Squabbles between the two titillated Louisianians.

Once a price had been set on Jean's head: 500 *piastres* (dollars). He replied with a duplication of the Governor's poster offering $1,500 to whomever would seize Claiborne and bring him to Grand Terre, Lafitte's headquarters on Barataria Bay. Another time it was said that Laffite, seeking a refuge from the police in a rich planter's residence, found himself facing Madame Claiborne. She was charmed by the manners and wit of that stranger introduced under an alias.

Later an event of prime importance would throw an even more favorable light upon Laffite, Humbert, and the human flotsam of the Haitian expedition. It was the Battle of New Orleans* on January 8, 1815.

How often Pierre Benjamin Buisson must have heard that battle described. "You, an artillery lieutenant, you should have been here! Your artillery men, Monsieur, they are the best in the world. They proved it during the Battle. Let me tell you about it."

One was expected to listen to the Orleanians as respectfully as school boys on the Paris street listened to veterans speaking of the Pyramids or the Lodi bridge.

* Usually referred to by New Orleanians as "the Battle."

This fight under the Chalmette oak trees, a fight which cost them only a few casualties compared to the enemy's heavy losses, appeared to the Louisianians as the Pyramids, Lodi, Austerlitz and Wagram all rolled into one.

Europeans wrapped up in the history of their own continent knew little about the war between England and the United States: Although the British had burned Washington the same year the Russians had set fire to Moscow in their resistance to Napoleon, the latter event was of greater importance to the French. When news of the English defeat in New Orleans reached the other side of the Atlantic, the Elba exile had landed at Cannes, and Europeans, either with terror or joy, were watching Napoleon and his ever-increasing little troop marching toward Paris.

"An ex-artillery officer! Congratulations! Would you like to hear what your comrades did here in January, 1815?"

What the French did would have astonished anyone less familiar with the Latin temperament than the Louisianians. With their Consul acting as spokesman, they insisted on their right not to be inducted in the army.

> Frenchmen,
> You will arm yourselves to defend a country who granted you a refuge when British intrigues had left you homeless. You will be fighting for people who have welcomed you as brothers and given you the right of citizens. Honor, patriotism, gratitude urge you to fight and I do hope this appeal will find you responsive.
> Humbert, Brigadier General

It was followed by a post-script stating that the volunteer corps would be commanded by French-speaking officers familiar with the tactics that so often had made them victorious in Europe.

Then, the "Frenchmen from France" en masse, the *Chant du Départ* on their lips, rushed to the combat.

Unexpectedly, General Moreau's name also came in for praise because fifteen years earlier he had pointed to a location to be fortified in case an attack came from the river. Hastily, Orleanians piled there sacks of earth and, according to some sources, cotton bales behind which they could stage an ambush. The erecting of this system of defense was supervised by a Frenchman, Major Lacarriere Latour, formerly Monsieur Latour de Lacarrière, a *cadet de Gascogne* who had learned much through his contacts with military engineers at San Domingo.

During the battle, among the heterogeneous group (Creoles, Kentuckians, Tennesseans, Baratarians, free men of color, Choctaws, Negro slaves) were numerous veterans from Leclerc's expedition. They were in charge of the cannons.

Some were under the command of the buccaneer Dominique You; others received their orders from a giant who had served under Generals Murat and Clauzel. He was Garrigues de Flaugeac, a Brigadier General in the Louisiana Legion and state senator. De Flaugeac was not one to remain shielded by his parliamentary immunity if there was a chance to fight. When this *cadet de Gascogne* found himself on a battlefield again, memories of Marengo and Haiti returned, along with his rage for humiliations suffered in English prisons. He was the first to fire a cannon, the others following suit. The advancing British were taken by surprise and the swamps reddened by their uniforms and their blood.

Everything was going according to plan on the eastern side of the river when a messenger arrived breathlessly announcing a rout on the west bank. Orleans might be caught between two fronts. An officer able to restore order and inspire courage was needed. Anyone later relating this incident would ask: "Do you know who was chosen?" After a pause the storyteller would exclaim: "Humbert!"

Impulsive Humbert did not wait for written orders, thereby encountering difficulties with the commandant on the other shore of the Mississippi. But the situation clarified. It did not take long for him, with his imperious manner and magnetism, to rally the soldiers. "Intrepid Humbert, former general of the French Republic, looked for death everywhere and could not find it," Bernard de Marigny wrote.

Meanwhile, from the Gulf of Mexico, Laffite and his men were watching the open sea to prevent British reinforcements. It is said that Laffite turned down a bribe (money and rank in the British army) offered to him, but he did so after a pretense at hesitation which gave him time to warn his countrymen of the incoming fleet. He who had been considered the most wanted criminal then offered his services to the Governor.

"Laffite is a great patriot!" the whole city exclaimed. As his only reward, he obtained a pardon for his younger brother, Pierre, imprisoned after being caught smuggling under the cover of his blacksmith shop.

In his Order of the Day after the battle, General Andrew Jackson praised the Laffites, mentioned the help furnished by Major Lacarriere Latour and Captain You, complimented Garrigues de Flaugeac and thanked Humbert who "exposed himself to the greatest danger with his characteristic bravery."

At the same time the Ursuline nuns thanked the Virgin for the protection given to their city; the English buried their dead under the oak trees; ladies leaned from their balconies to smile at the victors. The popularity of Bonaparte's soldiers climbed. They did not, however, keep out of trouble.

Martial law had been proclaimed. Bristling with anger, rebellious Frenchmen protested the restrictions. Their attitude could not be understood by Andrew Jackson, who soon ordered them, their Consul included, to leave New Orleans. There followed an immediate uproar. "To chase them away . . . after what they have done for us!" citizens complained. During the weeks of confusion which culminated in Jackson's being accused of usurping too much power, the Frenchmen appeared as victims and their prestige continued to increase.

The same could not have been said about their official representative. He was still the Tousac who served as Lieutenant-Colonel at San Domingo and became vice-consul in New Orleans. When the Empire fell for the first time in the spring of 1814, he continued to occupy his post as agent of Louis XVIII and found it apropos to use his *Ancien Régime* title and name. The chevalier Anne Louis de Tousac's tribulations were many. He had lost an arm on the battlefield and the refugees from the West Indies could testify to his bravery. But to forgive him for having become a turncoat was something else.

The importance of emblems, of colors—the color of a flag or a cockade—was considerable. Within fourteen months France saw the Empire give way to the Monarchy, then the return of the Empire, then the changing into a Monarchy again. Since news took almost three months to reach the delta, the bewildered Tousac was never quite sure of his decisions. But the fiery Bonapartists were always ready to remind him *they* did not approve of any change in allegiance.

During the summer of 1814, people walking on

Toulouse Street saw a sight that increased their bitterness. Two workmen were removing from the French consulate gate the Imperial eagle and replacing it with a *fleur de lys*. This change of emblems brought the realization of Napoleon's fall more vividly than all the articles of the *Courrier de la Louisiane*, the *Gazette de la Louisiane*, and the *Amis des Lois* together.

Shortly afterward passersby again stared at the gate, this time with a smile. The fleur de lys had disappeared, obviously carried away during the night. Authorities again replaced it with a marble slab tightly screwed to the framework. But nothing could prevent passers-by from vigorously hurling a hammer at the new emblem a few nights later.

Chevalier de Tousac appealed to Governor Claiborne for help in the matter. How troublesome the Frenchmen were, the Virginian must have thought. He remembered the time one of them had threatened the life of an anti-Bonapartist journalist. To pacify the Consul, Claiborne posted an offer of $200 as a reward for the arrest of the bandits who showed no respect for His Very Christian Majesty Louis XVIII's representative. The offer went begging.

For poor Tousac blows were coming from two sides, New Orleans and Washington. On June 9, 1815 he wrote to the Plenipotentiary Minister, Serurier:

> "I have the honor to inform Your Excellency of the arrival in this port of the boat "La Pauline," Captain Celluri. The arrival of this vessel caused a great excitement and placed me in a difficult position. This boat took a very long time to go up the river and the Captain was able to learn what had happened in France. The fear, should he enter this

harbor flying the white flag, to be insulted by the Emperor's numerous followers who already have manifested their feelings in excessive manners, has determined him to fly the tricolor. However, as he could not do without a certificate from the French consulate in order to obtain entrance, he came to us..."

Tousac continued in an apologetic tone, explaining that the captain might have done wrong but that circumstances were such that he, Tousac, did not have the heart to refuse the requested visa.

Once more the Consul was the target of criticism. When he mentioned the "excessive manners" in which Bonapartists expressed their feelings, he did not know yet what was in store for him.

The Emperor has returned! The magic words were being passed from one spectator to another in the little Theater St. Philippe. The Emperor has come back! The rumor grew. Sensing a strange agitation, the artists on stage stopped. Then Mayor Nicholas Girod, a native of Savoy, stood up and in a dramatic voice announced: "His Majesty has left Elba. If ever he should come to New Orleans I would be honored to offer him the hospitality of my home." The audience leaped up, shouting *"Vive l'Empereur!"*

News had spread through the city without anyone knowing from which newly arrived ship the news had come. "Mr. Mayor has offered his residence to the Emperor. What do you mean? Is he coming here?"

As everyone knew, Mayor Girod's home at the corner of Chartres and St. Louis Streets contained furniture, art objects, paintings imported from France and, more precious than anything else, a bust of Bonaparte. Was it a shrine for the fallen hero? Was it a home prepared for an extraordinary visitor? Tongues and imaginations were on the rampage.

Suddenly Pierre Caillou's voice was heard. Everyone could recognize that Gascon accent, the R's sounding like beats on a drum. Pierre Caillou, a bachelor and a bon vivant par excellence, spent most of his fortune dining and wining, especially wining his fellow countrymen. Any anniversary of Imperial victories was toasted *ad infinitum*. On this spring night, Pierre Caillou from Bergerac was in his glory. "Come on, fellows," Pierre told them. "I shall pay." A group rushed to the nearest Catalan's shop—a Catalan being a small grocery storekeeper, whether a native of Catalonia or not. Despite the late hour the merchant opened his door. Shelves, cases, cabinets were ransacked. "Don't worry, comrade, I shall pay," Caillou roared.

They took all the candles and dipped sticks in tar, in oil, in lard, anything that would burn. Lights were needed for the improvised parade. Sleepy citizens rushed to balconies. Frightened faces appeared through half-open shutters. "What is it? A flood? A fire?" "A fire again, yet the tocsin was not rung!" "Have the English come back?"

As the parade formed, its purpose became clear. Busts of Napoleon and Josephine were carried high amidst the flames and smoke of torches. Voices emerged through the uproar: "The Emperor has come back! *Vive l'Empereur!*" The crowd purposely passed in front of the homes of two Royalists. Their fists hammering a closed door, the demonstrators sang:

Monsieur Mazureau (Mr. Mazureau)
Dans son beau bureau (In his fine office)

White Cockade and Tricolor Flags 35

Comme un gros crapaud (Like a large toad)
Dans une baille d'eau (In a tub of water)

A short, heavy-set man, Mazureau, appeared for a brief moment at his second-story window. Had the little ditty familiar to urchins been inspired by its victim's appearance or by a distaste for his opinions?

Here was a man who condemned dueling in a city that relished this custom; here was a man who did not like Bonaparte. The lawyer Mazureau had arrived in New Orleans as early as 1801, letting it be known that a chance remark in a café about France's new dictator had caused him to be exiled.

The crowd stopped in front of the home of another lawyer, Dominique Seghers. Seghers had ceaselessly complained that Bonaparte was the cause of his financial troubles. While living in Antwerp he was responsible for the delivery of army supplies on a certain day at seven o'clock. The delivery was made at ten minutes after seven. Because of that lapse of ten minutes the supply officer had refused to pay the bill, although he had kept the goods. Seghers left Europe swearing that neither he nor any of his seven children would ever return to a country occupied by that tyrant who had never answered his appeal. Now the Flemish lawyer, always dignified, certainly would not face the hecklers. Noisily expressing their disapproval, the crowd moved on.

To the Consulate! Five hundred voices shouted down Royal Street. Turning the corner of Toulouse, they pushed open a gate and invaded the Consulate yard, pressing toward the gallery shaded by night jasmines.

French voices calling their Consul, Tousac thought. It is my duty to admit them. Calmly he appeared on the threshold. "The hat! the hat!" chanted the crowd. The hat, with its white cockade "large as a plate," had always exasperated the Bonapartists. What was the use for Tousac to put up a resistance? He gave an order. A half-awake slave with trembling hands offered the two-cornered hat. Eager fingers seized it. As pale as the cockade thrown at his feet, Louis XVIII's representative was forced to replace it with a tricolor ribbon.

"Cry *'Vive l'Empereur,'*" the crowd demanded. From Anne Louis de Tousac's tight lips a strangled *"Vive l'Empereur"* came forth. It was repeated hundreds of times by Pierre Caillou's followers.

Pierre Caillou then led the crowd toward his residence. In his yard, fragrant with piles of freshly cut lumber that had made his fortune, men sat on casks. There were always casks, full or empty. According to a witness, the *"orgies pantagruéliques"* lasted until eight o'clock the following morning.

"When did that happen?" Pierre Benjamin Buisson must have asked, interrupting the storyteller. "When? . . . Let me see. . . . It was a warm night . . . A very warm night. . . . It must have been the middle of June or shortly after." The ex-lieutenant winced. At the same time an obscure Belgian village had made history. Its name was Waterloo.

"How had Louisiana reacted to the news of Waterloo?" veterans falteringly asked sometimes. They could not know then about the learned Lakanal (who later would come to New Orleans), traveling toward the Western part of the continent with Pennières, a former member of the French Legislative Corps. Scouting for the location of a possible settlement, the pair found themselves facing a group of Osage Indians. When the strangers' nationality was revealed, the Indians exclaimed: *"Falanche Babichile Bonaparte! Bonaparte!"* Writing about this incident, Lakanal added: "What a man . . . . Waterloo defeat has not cooled off in the United States the enthusiasm for this prodigy of our century."

This remark would have been more true in Louisiana than anywhere else. Decidedly, the old Bourbon King with his velvet boots would not replace in Creole hearts Josephine's glorious husband. "What a weak, stunted style in all the writing of this government compared to the noble and majestic tone of the Imperial documents. This reminds us of Satan's gigantic companions who dwarfed themselves to enter the Pandemonium," the *Ami des Lois* wrote.

There were also personal animosities. In the months following Louis XVIII's Second Restoration, Monsieur Huchet de Kernion almost daily went from his Gentilly plantation to the harbor to watch the arrival of French boats. Would travelers be able to give him news of his young cousin Charles de la Bedoyère, whose gesture of welcome when Napoleon, returning from Elba, had reached Grenoble had started the Royal regiments' defection? The colonel knew that the Bourbons would not forgive him and already had sent funds to the United States where he planned to go. When would he arrive? With grim faces the *demi-soldes* answered that the colonel—no, the general, as a grateful Napoleon had bestowed this title upon him—would never arrive. Betrayed by a servant when he rushed to Paris to say goodbye to his wife and their newly born son, he had been arrested and sent to face a firing squad. Witnesses had dipped handkerchiefs in this new martyr's blood. The Huchet de Kernions wore mourning clothes and all the Creoles, being more or less related to each other, shared their grief. Thus, not only was the new regime without glamour; it also was without pity.

If Lieutenant Buisson had arrived a few months

earlier he would have met another Frenchman who would have enlightened him concerning the anti-Bourbon opinions of the city. Baron de Montluzin was one of those Ultra-Royalists who believed that Louis XVIII was not severe enough with the Emperor's former servants. He left Europe in disgust. Experiencing a rather cool welcome in Eastern cities, he decided to try his luck in the South. Unfortunately for him, his arrival in New Orleans coincided with the visit of two of Napoleon's generals: Count Lefebvre-Desnouettes and Baron Charles Lallemand. City officials entertained them, inviting at the same time General Humbert and another French newcomer, Taillefer. De Montluzin was indignant. That a concert be given in honor of those adventurers—Taillefer, a regicide, and Humbert, a drunk—was bad enough. But to think that on January 1 Governor de Villeré had called on them to offer official good wishes. That was too much! Was it not rumored also that this same de Villeré sometimes offered the hospitality of his home to Humbert when the wretched fellow was without lodging or perhaps could not find his way?

Bonapartists and Bonapartes seemed to pursue the unfortunate Baron everywhere. Upon entering the dining room of a charming Creole lady, whose portrait did he see? Life-size, in a Caesar costume, was none other than Joseph, ex-King of Spain, another member of that tribe who took pleasure in dethroning all Bourbons.

Had this irascible Ultra remained a few weeks longer he would have been enraged when the Théâtre d'Orléans presented *La Journée des Trois Empereurs* (The Three Emperors' Day), also called *La veille d'Austerlitz* (The Eve of Austerlitz). The performance furnished a fresh opportunity to boo the Bourbons while tricolor flags, springing up as if from a magician's hat, were unfurled on stage or brandished by spectators.

François Guillemin, who had replaced at the Consulate the pathetic loser of cockade and prestige, sent a report on the affair to his ambassador. This kind of agitation had exploded in other places. At the time of the first Imperial disaster, young lieutenant Philogene Favrot, in his usual bantering way, had written to his father, Colonel Pierre Joseph Favrot, better known as Don Pedro: "Baton Rouge politicos are going to pull their hair out when they hear of the fate of their God, Napoleon. I fear that the intrepid citizen Chardon may die of rage or lockjaw." There had been incidents also in Philadelphia and Baltimore, but in the Latin atmosphere of lower Louisiana, made still more Latin by the many settlers from Southern France, excitement assumed greater proportions.

The ambassador, Hyde de Neuville, a former *emigré* during the French Revolution, could understand the tension and restlessness caused by exile and did not want to be overly harsh. Yet it was his duty to mail strict instructions to all his consuls. Frenchmen from France knew they were being watched. Although irritating, it gave them a feeling of importance. Baron de Montluzin had stated that nowhere in the world would Bonapartists find people more favorably inclined toward them than in New Orleans. He was right.

At night in the Guillottes' courtyard the uprooted Parisian, Pierre Benjamin Buisson, upon hearing about events taking place in the community, wondered whether New Orleans deserved to be more than a temporary refuge. In the background, giggling girls with embroidery needles were tracing initials in the yuccas' fleshy leaves.

III

First Ties with the City

"NEXT WEEK, WE WILL TALK BUSINESS," Mr. Guillotte told Buisson. He advised his young cousin to let the festive season pass before attending to serious matters. The festive season celebrated on the grandest scale was New Year's Day, rather than Christmas. On January 1 visitors climbed the tall staircases leading to parlors. Young girls, curtsying, offered tiny glasses of liqueur red as rubies and rich with sugar. From the courtyard exclamations of delight were heard. Servants were running along the narrow gallery of the slaves' quarters showing each other a cotton dress or a shirt, gifts of the master.

The following day, calls were returned with the same punctuality and formality the ex-lieutenant had seen in Rennes or Metz.

Pierre Benjamin escaped that boring duty. It was so tempting to walk on the levee watching vessels arrive or to join comrades whose number was increasing daily. The taverns where the *demi-soldes* (by now they might as well be called the *sans-soldes*) gathered brought back the memory of the Caveau or the Café Lambertin of Paris with more variety in the accents.

"During the campaign of Egypt..." Maurice Barnett was saying. He had an English name but had not the *Grande Armée* been a real Babel?

First Ties with the City

"On the Lodi bridge . . ." and François Lambert began, launching into a story. Those men who had made the effort to pull up stakes and face a three-months' voyage into the unknown, however, did not sink into the quicksand of recollections.

In Louis Gally's home, for instance, contemporary matters claimed attention. The ex-artillery officer had married a Parisian just before his departure when he had felt that the *Lys* decoration awarded by Louis XVIII was not enough to buy his allegiance to the Bourbons. The wedding had taken place a month after Waterloo. The witnesses had been the father, an old sergeant just returned to civilian life, and Brutus, the younger brother. The extended honeymoon would take place in New Orleans, selected because the French language was understood there.

"Are you married also?" someone asked Victor Cherbonnier. The ex-brigadier of the 3rd Regiment of the Mounted Guard produced a document signed by his parents in the presence of a notary. It was his permission to marry; the name of the prospective bride would be added some day.

Buisson was asked what he planned to do. When he mentioned that he was a former Polytechnicien, he was assured of work. How lucky for Orleanians to find a well-trained engineer at home instead of having to import one from the North as was usually done. In turn, he asked how his fellow countrymen were getting along.

They were forced to search diligently to find work, offering their services through the gazettes. A great many clung to what often had been the newcomers' main skill: giving lessons. The Alsatian Montiasse had opened a *cabinet d'armes* where with flourishes and anecdotes he demonstrated the art of fencing. Porion, a former Cavalry captain, taught horseback riding. Numerous Frenchmen, in exchange for lodging, board, and a small salary, tutored the children of planters. Others having small capital and a wife to help them, opened private schools as aristocrat refugees from Revolutionary France or from San Domingo had previously done. Since 1727 Ursuline nuns had taken care of white girls (and Indians in another section), but in the growing city more schools were needed.

Bonapartist exiles arrived at the right time. Many became partners to Americans, each in turn giving instruction in his own tongue. Following the visit to the United States by the English pedagogue, Lancaster, his method of reciprocal teaching became a fad. It was especially suitable to New Orleans. Little Creoles were asked to correct the French spoken by the foreigners (Americans) and vice versa. "Students prefer studies of that kind to usual recreation," a master declared in a local newspaper.

Of course, all of these so-called educators were not equally prepared for their tasks. One day Buisson passed on the street a man whose features were familiar. How could anyone have forgotten this face cruelly scarred by smallpox? "Have I not seen you in Paris? Yes, I remember at Polytechnique, in a younger class. . ." Jean Baptiste Jeannin had just brought to the *Courrier de la Louisiane* a few lines announcing that he would teach "pure mathemathics in all its branches and geography including the use of globes." Buisson did not want to discourage his former comrade, but he wondered whether this scientific knowledge would appeal to the Orleanians as much as de Perdreauville's talent, for example.

De Perdreauville, a nobleman from Normandy, had been mentor (as was his official title) of Marie Antoinette's pages before he assumed the same function at the

Imperial court. He and his wife had opened an academy for young gentlemen and *jeunes demoiselles.* Colonel Cuvelier and his Louisiana bride began a similar school.

Unprejudiced Europeans also found a new field. In the local press one of them boldly upbraided the white fathers responsible for the life of octoroons, uprooted children who were disdained by the whites and disdainful of the blacks. "You, who stubbornly deprive such children of the advantages of a good education, fear the reproaches they will be justified in addressing to you some day," it was said. The school that was opened in answer to that appeal may have been responsible for the group of free men of color who became journalists and poets before the Civil War.

For a few veterans the new country was not the utopian America of their dreams. "Those dirty Englishmen, they bring nothing but trouble," mumbled Jean Claude Hudry, a merchant originally from Savoy. The fall of the Empire had left the British free to dispose of the merchandise accumulated during the blockade initiated by Napoleon. Cargoes pouring down in great quantities sold cheaply, leaving Hudry's shop without customers. "This is not the time to open a new store," warned the Savoyard, partly because it was true, partly because he did not want the number of his competitors to increase. But what an opportunity for some to assemble a pack of goods for resale! With a cart drawn by mules one merchant went to Mexico to sell silk and damask; another loaded a barge with precious objects and sailed upriver to Natchez where rich planters had acquired a taste for princely residences. More numerous were the less fortunate who searched the wharves for trinkets and glass beads which Indians would exchange for beaver or muskrat skins. To be a *coureur des bois* was not without danger, but danger was a challenge to some ex-soldier bored by city life.

Pierre Benjamin, as his comrades had said, perhaps with some envy, was better equipped than most of them. The ex-Polytechnicien could have taught mathematics. He loved working with numbers and hoped some day to measure the distance to stars. But astronomy was not remunerative and teaching did not appeal to him. He often heard that engineers were needed. At that time an engineer was also of necessity an architect, a contractor and a surveyor. New Orleans offered opportunities. It was bursting out of its three limits: Esplanade, Rampart and Canal Street. From the latter it overflowed toward St. Mary, as the American section was known, extending its flat facades and English-style windows, which the French called windows *à la guillotine*. The fourth frontier was the Mississippi River, and because it always threatened to flood, it had to be contained by the levee which needed constant supervision.

Architects were also in demand to repair damage caused by frequent fires. At the sound of the tocsin, volunteers put on bright uniforms, assembled in good order and generally arrived to gaze at smoking ruins. Flames broke out so often that the mayor, Count de Roffignac, an *emigré* from Revolutionary France, had organized a special corps of policemen to prevent arson. The American regime had not yet brought an end to destruction however, any more than the Spaniards who, at the end of the 18th century, twice had seen the river reddened by the glare of the burning town.

Buisson had to admit that he had a great deal to learn in his new country. The absence of stone was astonishing to him. Luckily, lumber was plentiful and not

First Ties with the City

too far distant. Under the direction of a foreman slaves molded clay and sand into bricks. Houses made of *briques entre poteaux* (bricks between beams) were erected and their geometrical designs covered with a pink or yellow lime mixture.

One also had to count on six months of a fiery sun baking the roofs, the walls and the outside staircases, changing the large drops of summer showers into steam. While working on plans, one had to consider the constant dampness of the soil permeated by the waters of the Mississippi and numerous lakes and streams and eroded by torrential rains. Trying to dig into that almost constantly muddy soil was frustrating, indeed.

There was always a Frenchman to exclaim: "*Mon vieux* (Buddy), impossible to have a good cellar here!" "What can you do with your wine?" "Drink it, comrade, drink it fast," any Pierre Caillou would answer. And someone might add: "They cannot even bury the dead here. They put them on shelves. Go to the St. Louis cemeteries. You will see."

The word *banquette* was not a misnomer. Sidewalks were raised like narrow benches above the overflowing gutters. Rich citizens rented their first floor to shopkeepers, and their lives were concentrated on the upper stories and in their patios where dry paths were provided by flagstones imported from Boston. Sometimes vessels brought blocks of stone as ballast. Yet, building was a challenge that Buisson would welcome.

An opportunity soon presented itself. The St. Louis Cathedral, named after a king of France, was majestic only in its name. Its flat roof between far-apart bell towers had a steeple almost as thin as a lightening rod. It made the façade look like a unicorn. The church wardens, a powerful group, succeeded in obtaining the civil authorities' good will, and it was decided that clergy and city would combine financial resources and give a better appearance to the Cathedral. Buisson submitted a plan. Unfortunately, he had a rival, Benjamin Henry Latrobe, thirty years his senior and already well known. Born in England, Latrobe had arrived in the United States the same year Pierre Benjamin was born in Paris. Latrobe had designed the Pennsylvania Bank of Philadelphia. In the same city he had established a system of water distribution, which was quite a novelty. New Orleans officials asked him to do with the Mississippi River what he had done with the Delaware. However, a lack of machines, which had to be imported from the North, hindered his efforts. In the meantime, Latrobe was rebuilding the Capitol in Washington, which had been burned by the British troops in the War of 1812. He sent his son to Louisiana. Young Henry had only time enough to supervise the construction of a hospital when yellow fever took his life. The father arrived and because of his reputation— and sympathy created by the death of his son—was given *carte blanche*.

The Municipal Council agreed, however, to give Buisson a chance to prove his talent. The city needed a new Custom House and had voted $82,000, a large sum for that time, for its construction. A much stronger foundation than the existing one was needed. The picturesque but frail Custom House they wanted to replace was a symbol of the difficulties the Spanish regime had encountered. A region more favorable to smuggling than the delta could hardly be imagined. Pirogues, canoes and barges at all times were hidden in some bend of the Mississippi or its tributaries, ready to glide toward the outskirts of the harbor and pile merchandise into carts. A curious ordinance had forbidden the greasing of wheels

First Ties with the City

so that their movement could be detected by the squeaking. Resourceful smugglers, however, had Negroes escorting them to hold buckets and pour water drop by drop on each axle. It deadened the sound and the silence was literally worth gold. Perhaps the new and better-staffed Custom House would usher in a more effective system.

Each day Buisson walked toward the river to watch bricks being piled up according to his directions. He wanted to do something as lasting as one would have done in Europe. He wanted to build for future generations. He had not yet learned that in his new country one planned only for a relatively short span of time. He could not guess that within twenty years New Orleans would become a far greater port and would require a much larger and impressive Custom House. But in 1819 Orleanians were satisfied with the result of Buisson's design, and the proud young architect now felt a kinship to his adopted city.

One could not always hope to be called to erect public buildings, but there were other tasks he could perform. The Place d'Armes, in the heart of the town, was surrounded by a delapidated fence. Buisson attracted the Municipal Council's attention to the matter and was successful in remedying the deplorable condition. He also worked for private individuals. No detail seemed too insignificant, and he brought to the execution of each one the same care French artisans gave to their work. Gazettes mentioned that Buisson had a certain secret calk able to stop rains from filtering through even the flattest roofs. He ordered marble mantelpieces from Italy to adorn Royal Street residences and rich planters' habitations.

Could these activities satisfy the dreams of a man who, in the Polytechnique quadrangle had discussed with his comrades how to fortify towns or build bridges for the

Grande Armée? He was wondering about it one evening when unexpectedly two callers came by. The two Creoles proudly talked about the part the Orleans battalion had played during the Battle. After that time it had become disorganized. It would be good to reactivate it and have other groups join it. "Would you accept, Sir, the responsibility of creating a corps of cannoneers?" he was asked.

Would he accept! Pierre Benjamin was elated. It could be a remedy to ward off bitterness and nostalgia. "Thank you, Captain, for accepting," his visitors told him. "You soon will receive your commission. Just give us time to have the Governor sign it."

The visitors had used the right word when they spoke of creating. Arms and men had to be conjured out of nowhere. Buisson soon became acquainted with red tape. Request after request had to be made in order to obtain for maneuvers a new cannon more effective than the old models that had stopped the British in 1815. Troubles were balanced by the pleasure of wearing a uniform and drilling men again. However, diplomacy was required.

"Will you ever learn to be on time?" the new Captain snapped at a nonchalant young man taking his place in a rank.

"Are you speaking to me?" the Creole retorted haughtily.

A furious Buisson dashed toward him. Quickly, bystanders intervened. It would not be well for the public to know about the incident.

Indeed, on Sunday afternoons the public would go to Place d'Armes or to Congo Square to watch the drill. The Napoleonic soldiers could be recognized by their military bearing and the eagerness they brought to their task. Orleanians would point them out to strangers:

First Ties with the City

ex-Colonel Vignié at the head of the Cavalry; Captain Buisson with his gunners; and the tall Louis Gally; and Cuvelier. The volunteers basked in the admiring glances. Pierre Benjamin felt that another tie had attached him to New Orleans.

"Any one who has drunk water from the Mississippi will come back for more," Alexandre Guillotte would tell his young cousin when the summer seemed unbearable, when fever made victims of his friends, when a traveler boasted of Mexico's better climate, or when a ship leaving for Europe would bring a longing to his eyes. "Go, if you wish, young man, but you will return."

Pierre Benjamin was staying. He had even sent for his brother Frederic. If Madame Buisson, afraid of bad encounters in wild America, could persuade her sons to remain under their relatives' wings, she would feel secure. No motherly advice was more obediently followed. It was not the Mississippi water that bewitched the Parisians, even if it was mixed with the orgeat syrup that Sophie or Elizabeth Guillotte offered them.

"Listen, *chère*," a lady would sometimes whisper in Mrs. Guillotte's ear, "I do believe that the Buissons are going to follow the Burthes' example."

Several years before, André Burthe d'Annelet de Rosenthal, during a brief and stormy stay in New Orleans, had the time to conquer Marguerite Suzanne Delord Sarpy's heart. He took her back to France and the sixteen-year-old bride, giving the lie to the Creoles' reputation for being languid, wore a lieutenant's uniform and became a member of her husband's staff when he was promoted to general. Monsieur d'Annelet, officer of the 4th Hussard regiment, as she was called, took part in several battles. When night fell on the Austerlitz battlefield she was riding at the side of the victorious Emperor.

When General Burthe was sent to Spain, she escorted him as far as Bayonne before realizing that it was time to bring this dangerous life to an end. Henceforth she devoted herself to the care of a large family while dazzling Parisian society with her charm and wit.

Perhaps it was her personality that gave another Burthe the idea to seek fortune and bride in Louisiana. Soon after his arrival in New Orleans, Dominique Burthe obtained the hand of Marguerite Suzanne's sister Louise. But Papa Delord Sarpy did not relish the idea of seeing another of his daughters leave for a far-away country. He pointed out to his new son-in-law the riches to be had without cutting virgin forest. Here they were in the form of Papa Delord Sarpy's endless cotton fields, piles of good timber and numerous slaves. Ex-lieutenant Dominique Burthe d'Annelet de Rosenthal, giving up country and career, became Mr. Burthe whose name in the census book was followed by the word "gentleman." He gave sensible advice to his fellow countrymen who met at the Charity Lodge where he became a 33rd degree Mason. Established in the Creole clan, he shunned adventurers. Monsieur Burthe represented one pole of society and General Humbert another.

Between the two, the Buisson brothers vascillated. Sometimes they felt satisfied in the home atmosphere of the Guillotte family. At other times, tired of the jasmin fragrance and orgeat syrup of the courtyard, they dreamed of new fields of adventure and escaped toward the Tremoulet Hotel.

IV

The Tremoulet Hotel

"WE, THE FRENCH, ARE NOISY PEOPLE!" Madame Tremoulet was saying at the top of her voice, strongly believing that the louder the words were spoken, the more intelligible they were to a foreigner. She was trying to entertain *Meester* Latrobe, one of the permanent residents of her hotel located at the corner of St. Peter Street facing the levee.

Where could the unfortunate Latrobe go to avoid that shrill voice? In the yard where so often a punished slave was moaning? On the terraced roof? From there, loud songs were coming: "Savages, we are French, have pity on our glory!" It was better to walk toward the Cathedral and supervise the erection of the new steeple, *his* steeple. As to his young rival, Buisson, he should forget about repairing churches and join his singing comrades.

Latrobe, perhaps spoiled by his success, spoke with contempt of the other Tremoulet guests. However, in one of them at least he could have found his equal. General Simon Bernard had served with distinction in Bonaparte's engineering corps. After Waterloo, he sailed for the United States, where he contacted his American colleagues and soon was held in great esteem in Washington.

He decided to apply himself to the improvement of communication in his new country.

In 1825, he tried to determine where a canal should be built to join Lake Pontchartrain to the Mississippi River. He selected the Chalmette section below the city as a proper site. But the time was not ready for this work. A road to be built toward Washington was considered a more urgent need. After the General left New Orleans to head the U.S. Engineering Department in Washington, the Orleanians did not forget him. They were pleased to hear in 1833 through their *Courrier* that Simon Bernard had been appointed aide-de-camp to King Louis-Philippe and General Director of the fortifications built around Paris. But at the Tremoulet, the studious and reserved Bernard had not attracted as much attention as the other French generals who stopped there whenever business or pleasure brought them to the big port.

Why were these generals in the United States? After Napoleon's fall, the loyal Bonapartists had to endure the Bourbons' resentment, especially if they had occupied a high rank in the Imperial army. On June 28, only ten days after Waterloo, King Louis XVIII issued a proclamation stating that he would not extend a pardon "to the instigators of that horrible plot," meaning the faithful subjects of the Emperor who had helped him to regain his throne upon his return from his Elba exile. Less than a month later a second decree singled out some generals accused of treason. Among them were Charles and Henri Lallemand, Lefebvre-Desnouettes and Clausel. Fearing the consequences of a trial and conviction of men considered as heroes, however, the government gave them time to flee.

On January 12, 1816 a law of amnesty was passed. But excluded from it were high ranking officers as well as

The Tremoulet Hotel 53

all relatives of Napoleon Bonaparte. Added to this was a paragraph which made many people fearful. The King reserved for two months the right to exile other suspects and deprive them of property and pension. The misery of the soldiers whose pay had been cut in half was a daily reminder of the contempt the new regime had for them.

Therefore, when the *Minerve Française* collected funds for the veterans wanting to settle in the New World, there were many claimants. But where would they go? Some of them gathered in Philadelphia and from there discussed the possibility of heading West. Two of them, Jean Pennières and Bazile Mestier, went scouting. Their first report was not favorable. While they studied the question another refugee, Colonel Nicholas Parmentier, was sent to Washington to petition Congress to grant a tract of land to the ex-soldiers anxious to "exchange sword for plough," as was their familiar expression. Where should this little colony be located? A Dr. Brown of Kentucky suggested the junction of the Black Warrior and the Tombigbee rivers in the Mississippi Territory, praising the sunny sky and the hospitable spirit of the inhabitants of Alabama and adjoining Louisiana. His advice was taken.

The following act was approved on March 3, 1817:

> "*Be it enacted by the Senate and the House of Representatives of the United States of America in Congress assembled,*
> That it shall be the duty of the Secretary of the Treasury, under the direction of the President of the United States, to designate and set apart, any four contiguous townships, each six miles square, of vacant public lands lying in that part of the Mississippi Territory, which was formed into a land district, by the act entitled 'An act for the ascer-

taining and surveying of the boundary line fixed by treaty with the Creek Indians, and for other purposes' "

In order to keep possible speculators at a distance, it was provided "that satisfactory evidence shall be produced that such agent or agents, are duly authorized to form such contract, and that the number of such emigrants, being of full age . . . are equal at least to the number of half sections contained in the four townships . . ."

A third section promoted the "cultivation of the vine and other vegetable productions as may . . . appear reasonable."

When Colonel Parmentier returned to Philadelphia, he gathered some companions and they left for Mobile, then a town of about 1,500 inhabitants living in wooden houses raised from two to four feet above the ground on large piles. When the schooner *McDonough* arrived, there was no quay where it could land. No doubt, to the veterans acquainted with European capitals, prospects must have seemed dim. But two beloved generals were with them, and they served to stir their courage.

On September 4, 1817 the *National Intelligencer* wrote: "Never was a project set on foot under better auspices . . . with more ardor and a fuller determination to make a fair experiment to show what Frenchmen can do." The article further quoted General Clausel, replying to someone surprised to see him enter such an apparently foolhardy expedition: "We have been accustomed to labour for the glory and happiness of our country, not to prey upon their or other people's necessities."

No doubt the brilliant Bertrand Clausel, who took such an active part in the Spanish campaign when trying to help Joseph Bonaparte to retain his Madrid throne,

The Tremoulet Hotel

showed compassion when he cast his lot with the refugees. It would have been so much easier for him to remain in the north in the vicinity of Bordentown where that same King Joseph, using the name Count de Survilliers, lived the pleasant life of a gentleman farmer.

An even more revered leader was Charles Lefebvre-Desnouettes. As a youth, he was Bonaparte's equerry, then became his aide-de-camp at Marengo and received the *Légion d'Honneur*. When the era of dazzling victories was declining, he fought in the arduous Spanish war, and in the Russian campaign. He was one of the officers Napoleon chose to accompany him when they left Moscow by sleigh, hastening toward Paris where the Imperial power was threatened. At the head of the light cavalry, Lefebvre-Desnouettes took part in the last campaigns and was at Waterloo. Upon the Emperor's return from Elba, Napoleon made him a lieutenant-general and bestowed upon him the title of count.

Ex-Lieutenant Buisson did not need an introduction to recognize Count Lefebvre-Desnouettes. He had seen him riding beside the Emperor on the battlefields at Brienne and La Rothière. He knew that the general was in the United States, but why in New Orleans? He soon received the answer. New Orleans was the commercial center where one could buy the tools and farm supplies necessary to clear off the banks of the Tombigbee River in Alabama where a group of *Minerve Française's* protégés had been sent. Occasionally Lefebvre-Desnouettes and his aide, General Clausel, who in Haiti had become interested in Southern cultures, came to make their purchases and stopped at the Tremoulet. What attracted the exiles to the inn probably was the flat roof overlooking the Mississippi. From there Lefebvre-Desnouettes watched the arrival of boats bringing news from France and with longing gazed at the departing vessels. His wife had remained in Europe and the greatest enemy the general had to fight was constant nostalgia.

Clausel and Lefebvre-Desnouettes devoted themselves to the aid of the Alabama refugees. But the man who officially served as President of the Société Agricole et Mécanique rarely set foot on the shores of the Tombigbee. This was the proud and bold Charles Lallemand. He and his meeker brother Henri brought an element of mystery to the inn, which might have been called the "Hotel of the Generals."

The careers of Charles Lallemand and Lefebvre-Desnouettes were quite similar. Both had been made peers during the Hundred Days as a reward for their loyalty to the Imperial regime. While Lefebvre-Desnouettes had been the Emperor's closest companion during the grim return from Moscow, Lallemand had been his most trusted aide after Waterloo. During the last hours of the reign he had desperately tried to persuade Napoleon to flee to America. Later, unable to obtain permission from the English to go to St. Helena and hunted by the Bourbons' police, he succeeded in crossing the frontier. He reached the United States after months of a fantastic odyssey reported in American newspapers: "General Lallemand is at Malta . . . He is at Constantinople . . . He has reached Russia . . . He is at Smyrna . . . He had landed in Boston." During all that time, worldwide attention was focused on him.

When Lallemand arrived in Philadelphia, he found his younger brother Henri already there, having been one of the first visitors to pay homage to Joseph, Count de Survilliers, at his Point Breeze estate. Henri, more polished than Charles, knew how to acquire influential friends. Charles shunned social life. He wanted adventures and men to command. The South would be good hunting ground, but not that tract of land where colonists dutifully would grow vine and olive trees and where the Choctaw Indians on the west bank of the Tombigbee would be peaceful neighbors. Such an enterprise would offer no challenge, he reasoned. Leadership of the colony soon was placed in the willing hands of Lefebvre-Desnouettes and Clausel.

Charles Lallemand's attention had turned toward Texas. He wrote the Spanish government requesting permission to choose the banks of the Trinity River as the location of the desired "asylum" or Champ d'Asile. The Spanish Bourbons did not deign to answer. Lallemand made another appeal. No answer. Assuming that "silence gives consent," he made plans to depart. In Paris the *Minerve Française* had raised funds. From Philadelphia the Lallemand brothers were gathering volunteers. A group embarked on the frigate *Le Chassepot* under the command of General Rigaud, hardly able to speak after a horrible throat wound. Napoleon had called him a martyr to glory.

While Henri lingered in Philadelphia courting a millionaire's adopted daughter, Charles joined the colonists and supervised their installation. Going up the Trinity River, they settled about seventy miles from the Gulf of Mexico.

"I will be back shortly, *mes enfants*," Lallemand told them. "Business calls me to New Orleans." And Lallemand appeared at the Tremoulet. He would climb to the roof to see if a new vessel had entered the port, then rush to the wharf and fire questions at the landing voyagers. He would accost captains and seamen, and he, a baron and peer, would invite them to shabby taverns and engage them in lengthy and hushed conversations. Watching longshoremen emptying ships' holds, he bought colorful glass trinkets treasured by Indians. He was said to have enquired where he could find 1,500 Bibles printed in "the language of Texas natives." Less openly, he negotiated the purchase of cases of guns and ammunition. It was rumored that he was on the lookout for cannon.

"Artillery lieutenant? Coming from Polytechnique? Indeed! If life becomes too monotonous for you here, let me know." Charles Lallemand's piercing eyes were challenging Buisson. Then abruptly he turned toward someone else. Buisson wondered. Why this question? Was it only to send one more man to Champ d'Asile? And why such a need of ammunition? Was the General's field of vision extending farther than the Trinity, toward that deeper part of Mexico from which Humbert had brought back stories at least as alluring as his Haitian tales?

What a temptation for adventurers to cross Louisiana's western frontier! Texas was part of Mexico, officially under Spanish domination, but the Royal family was held in such contempt that, in spite of the clergy's efforts, another form of government—any other form— would have been preferred. Parties fought each other without really knowing what their goals were. Politicians were always looking for condottieri. How lucky to have former Napoleonic officers within reach!

Humbert, with his big, childish handwriting, signed a commission offered him by a certain Manuel Herrera and headed for Vera Cruz in command of a filibustering expedition. At the Mexican port he delivered men and supplies to a Republican group. Upon his return, he stopped at Galveston as a guest of Jean Laffite at his Fort Rouge headquarters. Finding a pair of tarnished gold epaulettes and a plumed hat among the pirates' loot, he pompously assumed the title of Governor of Galveston.

The Tremoulet Hotel

For a time he reigned over sand, waves and bushes twisted by the wind and shared his sovereignty with the Gulf buccaneers. But when he returned to New Orleans aboard a frigate flying the Carthagenian flag and noisily entered the Tremoulet, the hopes of many restless exiles soared.

When Buisson began dreaming of adventures, there was always a voice calling him back to other duties or other plans.

"Captain, there is to be a parade tomorrow on the Place d'Armes. We count on you to be there."

"*Monsieur l'architecte,* could you come to my habitation? It has to be enlarged. Little Decima was born yesterday and my big sons are old enough to want a "*garconnière.*"

"Cousin, what are you and Frederic thinking about? You are not going to visit the Texan savages, are you? Cannibals would eat you up!" the Guillotte sisters said laughingly.

Pierre Benjamin was not the only person whose curiosity was aroused by Charles Lallemand's attitude. The *Gazette de la Louisiane,* not as favorably inclined toward the Napoleonic refugees as the other newspapers, was eager for any piece of information throwing light on the general's conduct. One day the *Gazette* reproduced a letter from Nakitosh (Natchitoches), a former post at the time French kings dotted their New World possession with forts. Nakitosh was located on the trail, also called Indian Trace, which connected many settlements and was widely used by *coureurs des bois,* always a good source of news. Through the grapevine a Nakitosh doctor had heard and reported in a letter to a Natchez colleague that "an extraordinary group of Frenchmen landed in Galveston bringing farm implements and arms

.... Three thousand more were expected. One did not exactly understand their intentions." The *Gazette*, reproducing the letter, emphasized the apprehension caused by these immigrants and their leader.

The leader, Lallemand, arrived in New Orleans just at that moment. He entered a *cabinet de lecture*, felt a certain coolness in the atmosphere, grabbed a *Gazette de la Louisiane* and stormed out to prepare an answer. The *Ami des Lois*, which published his reply, defended Lallemand while the *Gazette* stubbornly repeated in its next issue that this armed invasion was not in keeping with the peaceful promises frequently made by the General.

"I don't think too much of your Charles Lallemand," Guillotte would say to his young relatives who remained loyal to the Emperor's trusted servant.

Yet the day arrived when even Buisson's faith wavered. He was sitting with Louis Gally and a few other comrades in a Levee Street café. Suddenly a Frenchman named Crossiac, wearing the picturesque leather leggings and fur bonnet of the *coureurs des bois*, entered. He was followed by three Spaniards and an Indian guide.

Excitedly he asked the way to the French consulate. As soon as he entered Consul Guillemin's office his loud voice was heard through the closed door. Formerly a member of the Alabama colony, he had been sent to Texas and was anxious to let the French government's agent know what he had observed. The Tombigbee settlers complained that Charles Lallemand had compelled them to sell the piece of ground allotted to each one and send the money to Champ d'Asile. Moreover, some men had left Philadelphia convinced that their destination was Mobile, as the inscription on their baggage clearly showed. Yet, once they arrived in Mobile, the captain was paid a thousand-dollar bribe to keep his passengers on board, sail across the Gulf and land at Galveston.

Under the protection of the United States, the Alabama Vine and Olive colony (Société Agricole et Mécanique) offered to many exiles the security for which they were yearning. Men, land, money—the general thought he was free to dispose of everything! Would not the French Consul interfere?

Guillemin could offer only his sympathy. After all, the objectors were not prisoners. Their leader was no longer among them ready to coerce or punish; he was in New Orleans, and if Monsieur Crossiac wanted to deal with him directly he had only to wander through the port or climb up to the Tremoulet terrace. But why was Crossiac so sure that the Tombigbee was the ideal refuge? Alabama settlers were flocking to New Orleans, and their tales were not going to persuade people to replace them there.

"When are we going to drink your homemade wine?" This question addressed to anyone coming from Marengo County, Alabama, received only an evasive answer: "Later on. It takes time for grapes to ripen in this devil of a soil!" Even the enthusiastic Clausel who had figured that New Orleans would furnish an outlet for his protégés' crops had ceased smiling when someone would suggest: "Pierre Caillou won't need to import his favorite drink from his Gascony. Next August 15 we will celebrate the Emperor's feast with Alabama wine!" The time when Clausel or Colonel Raoul would proudly supervise the unloading of barrels from the Société Agricole seemed indefinitely postponed.

At first the Tombigbee colonists were light-hearted.

Several of them had brought their wives, who unpacked dainty dresses without the faintest idea of what pioneer life meant. Wooden cabins were built while a city was being planned. The men hunted, fished and worked with moderation. At night there was guitar or harp playing and dancing on the bank of the river. Sometimes a *farandole* climbed to the top of the white cliff from where one could see Choctaw fires in the distance. The first shock was to learn that the foundations of the dreamed-of city, Demopolis, had not been erected on the space granted by the United States government. New efforts were required to salvage bricks and beams and begin building anew. The *demi-soldes* named the second capital Aigleville. Eagles who had led them to victory in the past would certainly protect them. But more than symbolic eagles was needed.

These men who had engaged in military activities since the age of seventeen or eighteen and came from many different climates knew little about vine and olive culture. They showed little inclination to dig into the burning clay during the long hot summers. No one, with the exception of Lefebvre-Desnouettes, had enough money to acquire slaves, and most would have hesitated to do so. Had not Charles Lallemand told them once that at Champ d'Asile even the higher-ranking officers handled shovels and pick-axes? True children of the Revolution, they hated the institution of slavery, at least for the time being.

The growing of the vine presented special difficulties. Plants imported from France often arrived half dead. The space allotted to them in Marengo County, a name given by the French soldiers, was too low. Springs were scarce and stagnant pools left by overflowing streams bred mosquitoes and caused malaria. Numerous were the graves dug in the vicinity of Demopolis.

Unaware of those difficulties, another small group of French people cast their lot with the original settlers. They were belated refugees of the San Domingo disaster who, about 1820, tired of being tossed from place to place and hoped they might find success in Alabama. Some of the intended settlers never arrived on the banks of the Tombigbee. Some found themselves in Texas, rather than Mobile. Marshal Grouchy and one of his sons defaulted.

Loyal servants of the Empire had not forgotten an often repeated story about Grouchy. In the last and crucial phase of Waterloo, Grouchy resisted General Gerard's urgent request to rush badly needed help in the direction of the fighting and peacefully finished his dish of strawberries. Once in the United States, he lingered for a while in the cosmopolitan atmosphere of Bordentown where he did not encounter much hostility and sent his son Victor to take care of his allotment in Alabama. A member of an old aristocratic family, Count de Grouchy may have sensed that the life of a pioneer would not satisfy his tastes.

The colonists were discouraged but too proud to admit it. As an answer to their prayers, German immigrants appeared. Their offer to help was welcomed. They tackled the task with such vigor that the owners soon realized that their possessions were changing hands. In other cases, creditors, tired of waiting too long for delayed payments, seized the land. Furthermore, a group of American squatters caused ceaseless wrangling over land ownership.

A report sent from Aigleville in 1827 by Frederic Ravesies, "agent of the Tombeckbe Association" gives a heart-rending account of the hardships encountered by the settlers. As General Lefebvre-Desnouettes' strenuous efforts to obtain further aid from Washington had come to naught, they began to leave. Some returned to France, taking advantage of a new amnesty; others made their homes in Mobile, New Orleans or Florida. Many years thereafter only silvery leaves of olive trees served as a reminder of the adventurous French soldiers.

Well-informed people in the United States were irritated, not only because of the sympathy for the Napoleonic refugees, but because their government's generous gesture (selling land at two dollars an acre without interest and with fourteen years to repay) had only enriched speculators in spite of the precautions taken. A Northern newspaper, *Niles' Weekly Register*, as early as the summer of 1818 spoke of the Alabama enterprise as "one of these splendid follies which amuse at certain times part of the American public."

In New Orleans, it was learned that Colonel Nicholas Raoul, who had been one of Napoleon's companions during the Elba exile and had led an advance guard of two hundred grenadiers during the march from Cannes to Paris, had given up his frustrating efforts. His wife, the former Marchioness de Sinabaldi, once a lady-in-waiting to Napoleon's sister, Queen Caroline of Naples, attracted customers to the inn they opened, thanks to her fabulous pancakes. With the help of the de Sinabaldi children, they took charge of a ferry across French Creek, three miles east of Demopolis. This work proved too monotonous for Colonel Raoul, however, and in 1824 he went to Mexico where a chance to fight was always at hand. When he died he was Governor of Toulon, France.

General Count Bertrand Clausel preferred a vegetable garden near the Bay of Mobile to his land on the

Tombigbee and did not mind bringing his products to market by himself. But in 1825, he received permission to return to France and a few years later King Louis Philippe appointed him governor of Algeria.

But Lefebvre-Desnouettes would not give up. In a desperate gesture, he sank $25,000 he had brought from France in the undertaking. From his log cabin made into a shrine to his Emperor, he described the colonists' troubles in his letters to his wife. She was related to the Parisian banker Jacques Lafitte, who sent money, but it was too late.

Wrapped in melancholy, Charles Lefebvre-Desnouettes traveled from Mobile to Philadelphia, birth-place of the association instrumental in choosing Alabama for the ill-fated venture, and thence from Philadelphia to New Orleans. Exile erased ranks. He and Clausel mixed freely with other clients of the Tremoulet Hotel, and through them the whole city knew of the veterans' misfortune.

One day the ex-soldiers hastily climbed down from the terrace to witness another disaster. A frigate flying the Carthagenian flag was entering the harbor. Curious eyes watching from the levee could read the vessel's name: *San Antonio de Campeche*. It had been mentioned in a letter printed by the *Gazette de la Louisiane*. It was Jean Laffite's latest and biggest catch in his war against the Spaniards, a 450-ton frigate with a cargo worth $360,000. Had they emptied their loot at Grand Terre, or would there be silk, jewels, and amber-colored wine in Pierre's blacksmith shop tonight? The news spread and from the nearby market merchants and buyers, interrupting bargaining and gossiping, rushed to the wharf.

They saw a wretched group coming down the

gangway, including six women and as many children. Their leader was an elderly man with his jaw and throat horribly mutilated. Immediately, he was recognized as General Rigaud.

"General Rigaud! Then, Champ d'Asile comrades must be coming!" The words flew from café to shop, reaching Montiasse's fencing school, Porion's Riding Academy, Cuvellier's pension, Buisson's office. Everyone left half-filled glasses, purchases, swords, horses, pupils or drawing boards and raced to the port.

When they saw the grim faces of the passengers silently disembarking, the Frenchmen took off their hats and saluted. There were 77 of them, led by the pathetic Rigaud walking with an effort, assisted by his son and daughter. Once more Orleanians showed their hearts and opened their homes to them. After recovering somewhat, each of the refugees described with bitter words the collapse of Champ d'Asile.

First, they had sent to relatives and friends glowing descriptions of Texas: the beauty of the trees, the abundance of game and the size and color of birds unknown in Europe. Indians were always willing to offer a peace pipe and senoritas were alluring. The tasks of clearing the forest and setting up a camp had been performed with gusto.

It was a beautiful camp, according to the colonists, with bastions at each angle, the powder house in the center, two large cabins for the generals, and little gardens around the quarters reserved for Dr. Viole and his family and for Mademoiselle Rigaud. From reveille to curfew the veterans drilled; little time was left to cultivate the land. General Rigaud was hardly heard, of course, but Lallemand bellowed orders from one end of the settlement to the other.

Lallemand had succeeded in making such an impression on the Indians that after passing him the peace pipe, they had placed a feather headgear on his bushy dark hair and had named him their Great Chief. At night, the soldiers formed a circle, kept branches burning to repel bears, panthers, snakes and mosquitoes, and until dawn listened to Lallemand speaking about their Emperor. "If *he* had listened to my suggestion, *he* would be in America. . . . If *he* were here . . . If *he* should ever arrive. . . ." There was always someone to ask: "After all, would it be impossible?" Fantastic plans were outlined.

Then the General would disappear. His presence was missed. The forest then seemed more threatening, Indians and Mexicans less friendly, nights more endless. Narcisse Pericles Rigaud interpreted his father's orders, but this voiceless chief hardly seemed a protector. Why were all these cases of ammunition arriving at Champ d'Asile? Had not the *Minerve Française* printed this statement: "Frenchmen settling in Texas are bringing there the fruit of civilization. . . . No feeling of greed accompanies them. . . . All they ask from Heaven and men is the enjoyment of land and water, freedom, working days and peaceful nights"?

Lallemand had signed this declaration. Yet his activities in America were not in keeping with it. The settlers were not the only ones to feel uneasy. One day a troop of five hundred Mexicans marched against them. They were followed by Spanish regiments from San Antonio. Fearing for the fate of the women and the children, General Rigaud advised that they yield to the Mexicans' demand and evacuate the camp. Where was Charles Lallemand in this hour of need? In New Orleans, of course.

For days, through underbrush and swamp, the disheartened and half-starved men made their arduous way toward Galveston. They reached it just as a gigantic tidal wave washed the island. Reduced in number, the group clung to bushes twisted by the wind. In the distance they saw silhouettes approaching. Through lips burned by salt and the sand came the cry: *"Au secours!"* (Help!) Then, above the turmoil, a French voice was heard shouting: *"Tenez bon, les enfants, on arrive!"* (Hold on children, we are coming!) A giant in an outlandish uniform, ruddy face under a grey mane, gesticulating and roaring orders, towered above them. The refugees of endless disasters thus became acquainted with General Humbert.

Proudly he introduced himself as the Governor of Galveston, and with his picturesque retinue compassionately guided them toward Jean Laffite's headquarters. After a few days of rest and good treatment they were invited to board the *San Antonio de Campeche.*

Thus ended Narcisse Pericles Rigaud's tale to Buisson, Gally, Charles Lavaud and other comrades. As he finished his story a noise was heard at the door. General Charles Lallemand was entering as if blown by a tempest— his usual manner. The men sitting at the tables remained seated. They did not salute. "Where are the others?" Lallemand asked harshly. "Where is Pennières? Where is Héritier . . . and Hartmann . . . and Milliard?"

Silence shrouded the room. Narcisse Rigaud stared at Lallemand, resentment in his eyes.

V

Turmoil and Fever

THE OTHER COLONISTS ARRIVED, at least a few of them, clothes in rags, feet wrapped in bandages, faces swollen from insect bites. When by great effort they were able to speak they added to the Champ d'Asile stories. Chenet was the only survivor of an overloaded skiff that had capsized. Another veteran had even a more gruesome tale. Once, near a camp fire abandoned by Indians, the Frenchmen had come across pieces of uniforms, and they thought they recognized faces half eaten by beasts.

When some fugitives were crossing the Sabine River to enter Louisiana they met Just Girard, who was going back to Texas in the company of other travelers. He said that while he was hunting, his mustang had followed a herd of wild horses. After an hour of furious riding he had fallen to the ground. Regaining consciousness he saw Indians surrounding him. He remembered advice given by a *coureur des bois*: "The Comanches hate Spaniards. In case of danger, make them understand that you are French." Girard opened his coat. Pinned to the lining was his Legion of Honor cross. He pointed to it and said: "Napoleon!" The Indians repeated the name with awe. Girard became for them a sort of god, and they would not let him go. It was months before he could escape. Then why was Girard going back to Texas? He and others like him had acquired a taste for adventures that the land west of the Sabine might satisfy.

"The Laffite brothers gave us proof of a most touching interest," said the ex-colonist Héritier. They must not have found it too hard to find some new recruits from among the ranks of the veterans. Grand Terre, Grand Isle, Timbalier Island, Barataria—the names sounded like a call to battle. Intoxicated with freedom after years of army discipline and greedy for action, loot and captives, some soldiers joined the buccaneers without remorse.

Others had only one desire, to return to France. But among them were the timid hearts, afraid to face people at home who had warned them that America would not be a paradise. And there were some who did not want to render useless the sacrifice they had made when they uprooted themselves.

Among Orleanians, friendly greetings and generous gestures were followed by uneasiness. After a few months, the *Courrier de la Louisiane* begged the Governor to publish a letter known to have been received. It contained the *Minerve Française*'s promise of financial help. The Paris newspaper, alerted to the colonists' plight, felt partly responsible for the abortive Alabama and Texas ventures. Governor de Villeré acted with caution. This piece of news, if suddenly spread, might bring to his office more or less legitimate claimants. He requested Charles Lallemand to make a list of his protégés. This task did not appeal to the General and he passed it on to Pennières who, stopping in Texas in the course of his travels, had become Lallemand's right arm. While Pennières made a round of all the places where the refugees might be lodging, de Villeré formed a committee to attend to the distri-

Turmoil and Fever

bution of the funds. He appointed the lawyer Moreau-Lislet, a great admirer of the Code Napoleon,* François Xavier Martin, a thrifty judge from Marseilles, Colonel Zenon Cavelier, who had praised the *furia francese* during the Battle, and the rich planter, Nicholas Destrehan. All of them were intelligent, honest and compassionate.

After much delay the committee announced that each Champ d'Asile settler would receive from $40 to $200 according to his rank and his needs. Citizens were asked to notify the government through the press if they knew of any error. Young Rigaud protested that he was not a lieutenant, but a captain: "If *Monsieur le Général* Lallemand had not considered me as a captain, without any doubt he could not have promoted me to the rank of major as he did by virtue of the authority granted to him by the Mexican Republic." So, in spite of his denial, the General had actually taken part in Mexican internal struggles.

Narcisse Rigaud's complaint may have been inspired by his pride or by a desire for justice, but not by greed. The veterans unanimously had decided first of all to offer a reward to Humbert and then to share the donation equally, with the exception of the two generals who would receive more money. Lallemand in a grand gesture refused his 5,500 francs, and his protégés in another *beau geste* gave this sum to the poor of St. Louis Cathedral.

Sentimental Creoles were pleased, with one exception. Lallemand, finding the Tremoulet not private enough to conduct his interviews, had rented a little

---

* The civil code adopted in March, 1808 in Louisiana was largely based on the Code Napoleon instituted in 1804. In spite of a few changes in 1825 and later, it has remained in force.

house downstream. The owner, de Fériet, was not satisfied with his tenant. He complained to his sister that "this rascal (Lallemand), who in December 1819 had finally bought for $12,000 the little farm (slaves included) which he had rented up to that time, failed to make his payments." De Fériet was surprised since he knew of "large sums" his tenant had received from unnamed persons. What did he do with all that money?

Other people also wondered. The city soon divided into pro-Lallemand and anti-Lallemand factions, and the gazettes plunged eagerly into the battle. Pennières and a veteran named Lagarde were nicknamed the "Don Quixotes of the Champ d'Asile" by indignant comrades who reminded them that they, Lagarde and Pennières, had been among the first to protest against "the blows distributed by the fist . . . of the idol of their heart to the unfortunate men . . . he had dragged into the Texas desert."

The publisher of *L'Ami des Lois* was Pierre Cherbonnier, a Frenchman who, although he had been for a few months Jean Laffite's secretary at Grand Terre, was nevertheless a peaceful citizen. Entangled in controversy, he was sued for slander. Unable to pay, he was sent to prison, according to custom. Friends bailed him out but the number of Lallemand's enemies had increased. Another Frenchman, distressed by this quarrel, tried to establish unity but was advised by the press to mind his own business. Who could believe that in spite of all this Gallic uproar New Orleans' most popular play in the spring of 1820 was *"Les Grenadiers Français"* (The French Grenadiers), with music by Gretry?

The ex-soldiers were to suffer another shock when they read that General Humbert had been sent to the Calaboose, the prison whose dark and narrow cells opened on the Cabildo's courtyard. Usual tenants were fugitive

Turmoil and Fever

slaves, whose head and hands were pinned in stocks, as well as arsonists and thieves. Pierre Laffite had stayed there from the end of 1814 until Jean's heroism won his pardon. But why had Humbert, with his glorious past, been arrested as a common criminal?

The answer circulated through the city. A few months before a man named Desfarges, accused of an act of piracy committed in the Gulf of Mexico, declared that General Humbert had given him the commission which made him a privateer. If only Humbert could be located, Desfarges would be cleared of the charge. Where was Humbert? In spite of their protests Desfarges and a few of his sailors were hanged. Hardly had this tragic incident been forgotten when another sprang up. This time two Frenchmen claimed that they held *lettres de marque* signed by a certain Humbert. The report added that the signer "illegally took the title of Governor of Texas," assumed some fictitious power, and had "aided, abetted and commanded" the culprits.

Just at that time Humbert returned to New Orleans. Elated by the gratitude of his protégés, he made his boisterous presence seen from tavern to tavern. "Well, *mes enfants*, how lucky you are," he told them. "The tidal wave did not swallow you up!"

His subsequent arrest drew mixed reactions. The Creoles withdrew their sympathy. Piracy had touched too close to home. Jewels belonging to a lady who recently had sailed out of New Orleans had been found among those auctioned off by the Baratarians. Many Frenchmen were beginning to find Humbert's conduct somewhat embarrassing. Yet the old warrior was in prison, "perhaps chained like a criminal . . . having for his only food dark bread soaked with bitter tears." Help should reach him.

Curiously enough, this help came from strangers. The Second District (the American Section above Canal Street) through its senator secured legal advice for the prisoner. *L'Ami des Lois* also came to the rescue, declaring that the General's only mistake had been to trust the Mexican Republic "where crime and virtue unfortunately were often taken for each other. Carried away by his devotion to democratic principles the former servant of the French Revolution had protected bandits, mistaking them for patriots fighting the Spanish tyranny. . . . A motive stronger than the thirst for gold has always inspired Humbert's acts." Since the judge who had sentenced him was relaxing at Pensacola "eating oysters and drinking light wine," who would open the old lion's cage?

The Governor himself put in a good word for Humbert. Governor de Villeré had no love for the Spaniards, whose ships allegedly had been plundered, as his father was one of the six Creoles trapped and condemned to die by the Spanish Governor O'Reilly. He also shared Humbert's hatred of the British. The prisoner was released and returned to his humble lodging on Casa Calvo street not far from his beloved cafés.

Humbert's cool jail cell in the Calaboose might have been a safe place. The summer had brought its wave of fevers. "Captain, you will have to fire the cannon tonight," was an almost daily command. Buisson knew what it meant. It was believed that the scent of gunpowder, together with the odor of tar burning at every street corner, helped to destroy germs.

"Yellow fever especially attacks newcomers, be careful!" visitors were told. But Benjamin (he now used only one Christian name) did not think of himself as a newcomer. He worried, however, about the comrades who were struggling through their first Louisiana summer. Several doctors had come from Champ d'Asile. One of them, Eudes de Gentilly, was full of good intentions but acted without diplomacy. He decided to give the Orleanians lessons on the touchy subject of hygiene. Dirty water running along the *banquettes,* cisterns in which bird droppings and dead pigeons floated, choked up gutters and piles of trash needed to be cleared away. Orders to destroy the clothing of victims were ineffectual since strips of burning material carried by the wind were allowed to fall into courtyards and on balconies. No one listened to Dr. Eudes. Then he offered a remedy guaranteed to cure 95 patients out of 100 if only the State of Louisiana would grant him financial help. "Let him cure first and we will pay later," was the answer. Discouraged, Eudes de Gentilly left New Orleans. Other doctors of the Napoleonic era remained and their devotion created for them strong ties with their adopted city.

"*Mossieu Docto.*" A Negro child was pulling Felix Formento's sleeve. "*Mossieu Doctor, ti Doctor Fomento?* Please, *vini.*" How often he and his colleagues had been called to see a patient and then had to return hurriedly to attend to some other member of the household. But why did the Negro boy want him especially? It was useless to ask questions. Answers would come in an unfamiliar patois—half French and half African. The doctor and this young guide turned the corner of St. Philip Street and entered a low house. A servant silently led the way toward a bed. Formento did not recognize the patient, yet the voice, although low, was somehow familiar. He had heard it once, loud and vibrant over the tumult of waves. It was Jean Laffite!

Jean Laffite had called for him because he remembered the surgeon's devotion to his comrades during the

Galveston drama. But what the feverish man wanted most of all was for the doctor to rush toward another sick person. With effort, he gave an address. Formento left. On the Place d'Armes he passed Buisson supervising his cannoneers in firing a big gun at regular intervals.

"Does this do any good?" the young officer asked, his face damp and dirty with sweat and powder.

"It gives them a little hope! What a summer! What a city! Are you going to remain here forever?"

"I don't know, but *you* should stay. Doctors are badly needed."

"Engineers also. In a few months there will be another threat." Formento was pointing to the Mississippi.

The woman who opened the door of the second home was a handsome octoroon. "Where is the patient?" The patient was an adolescent girl with a white face and large dark eyes which reminded Formento of Laffite.

A few weeks later the same little Negro guide came for him again. Had the yellow fever returned to the same home? Not very likely. Usually it killed fast or else gave a respite until the next summer. Perhaps it was only malaria this time.

No, the great buccaneer only wanted to pay his debt. Formento stopped him. Champ d'Asile men owed too much to their Galveston savior. Laffite insisted: "Gold is not enough to reward the doctor who saved me...and my child. Ask for anything you want, *Monsieur* Formento." Laffite was looking at the young girl—so white. But whatever the skin's whiteness, Creoles would never forget this sixteenth of other blood. She would be *placed,* meaning that at the Octoroons' Ball she would meet a rich planter, and perhaps become his mistress. He would give her a tall mansion on Rampart Street, jewels, carriages, slaves and children—many children—but never his name. A Euro-

Turmoil and Fever 77

pean would not have the same prejudices, not even aristocratic Formento from the Turin Academy and the *Grande Armée*. According to the French custom, Laffite's daughter would receive a dowry made up of the treasures piled up in the Fort Rouge or at Grand Terre.

"I will give you anything your heart desires, Doctor. You just have to ask..."

The girl had left the room. Formento smiled. During the long trek to New Orleans a young widow, near Boutte, had proved hospitable to him. Lower Louisiana was under the sovereignty of the Baratarians who seldom let strangers enter their land. But Laffite's name had a magic power.

"Please, all I want is a passport to go to see my fiancée." Coldly, Laffite assented.

Fevers were still raging. Buisson learned that one of the Tremoulet guests, his rival, the architect Latrobe, was dying from the same disease which had killed his son. Fever attacks mostly the newcomers, Guillotte had warned, therefore the Champ d'Asile group was to furnish some victims. Urbain Renou died. He was one of the signers of the violent letter against Lallemand which had resulted in having Cherbonnier sent to jail. He lived beyond the city limits on a little farm where he grew indigo and sweet potatoes, a peaceful occupation for someone who loved to relate his campaigns in Spain and in Russia. Poor Boyé would be buried in Louisiana soil also far from his native Figeac.

The cruelest loss for the veterans was General Rigaud's death. Although he disapproved of Lallemand's conduct, Rigaud always tried to avoid all dissension. Orleanians had learned to look with respect at the disfigured face. The *Courrier de la Louisiane*, reviewing his career, ended an obituary with these words: "As many other brave men he was waiting for a chance to serve his country again."

The journalist had been right. The Frenchmen were waiting for the moment, not to serve their country, but the man who symbolized it in their eyes—Napoleon. Probably this uncertainty and expectation were responsible for the constant agitation that often irked the Orleanians. For the ex-soldiers, in spite of links which day after day tied them to their surroundings, Louisiana would be considered only a temporary shelter as long as the St. Helena prisoner was alive. As long as he was alive, on the Tremoulet roof, at *Le Veau qui Tête* (The Suckling Calf), at Thiot, Turpin, or the Café Napoleon (there was one by that name), veterans would whisper of their hopes and their plans.

The Royal Consul, François Guillemin, was worried. He had learned that in New York the well-known refugee Regnault de St. Angely had revealed during a serious illness a plan to kidnap the Emperor. Was the man delirious? There was something more tangible than the dream of a sick man. In Washington, a bundle of documents had been seized that greatly worried both Hyde de Neuville and his Spanish colleague, Luis de Onis. The papers referred in detail to a Confédération Napoléonienne. The goal was to have Joseph Bonaparte, then in Philadelphia, recognized as King of Mexico and other possessions in the New World. The Count de Survilliers was a peaceful man. He was so devoted to his brother that he offered to take his place when the *Northumberland* was about to sail for St. Helena. Obviously Joseph, for whom reigning in Spain had been a detestable chore, would gladly pass the Mexican crown to Napoleon should a kidnapping be successful. The papers were not signed, but through a seal their origin could be traced to one of

Lieutenant Pierre Benjamin Buisson of the 6th Artillery of the Grande Armée, one of many Napoleonic exiles who found a new life in Louisiana. An engineer, Buisson designed the New Orleans Custom House.

(Courtesy Louisiana State Museum)

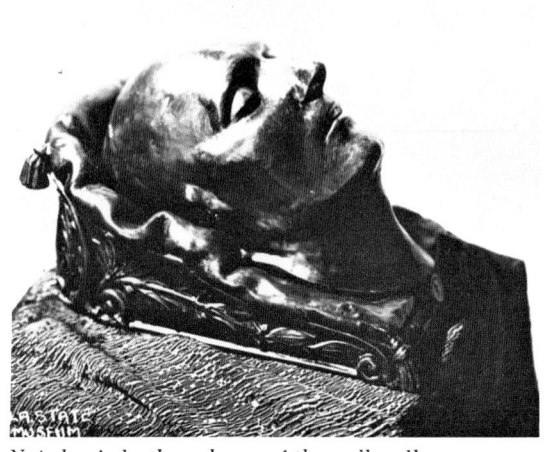

Napoleon's death mask, one of three allegedly made by Dr. Francesco Antommarchi, the Emperor's personal physician on St. Helena, was given to the people of New Orleans by Dr. Antommarchi. Lost in the aftermath of the Civil War, it eventually was restored to its place in the Cabildo, now the Louisiana State Museum.

(Courtesy Special Collections Division, Tulane University Library)

Dr. Francesco Antommarchi, controversial physician who ministered to the Emperor in his dying years. Dr. Antommarchi later practiced medicine in New Orleans but eventually was rejected by the people of the city.

(Courtesy Special Collections Division, Tulane Library)

The old Spanish prison, located within the historic Cabildo in New Orleans, was referred to by the French as the Calaboose. The prison has housed such notable figures as Pierre Lafitte and General Humbert.

(Courtesy Louisiana Collection, Special Collections Division, Tulane University Library)

View from the roof of the Tremoulet Hotel, one of the favorite gathering places of Napoleonic exiles in New Orleans. The high-roofed building in the center is the Government House. Jefferson Street is at the far left.

(Courtesy Louisiana Collection, Special Collections Division, Tulane University Library)

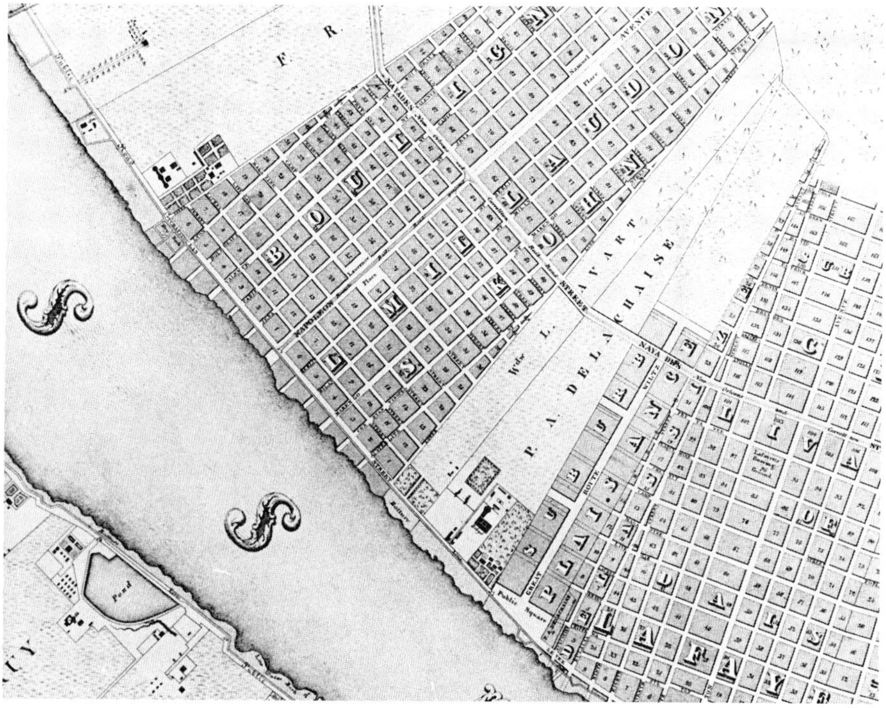

This portion of a map drawn by Charles F. Zimpel in 1835 shows Napoleon Avenue as it leads away from the Mississippi River, separating Faubourgs Bouligny and Millaudon.

(Courtesy Historic New Orleans Collection)

(Photograph by Edgar Shore)

This is a copy of the certificate which, along with the St. Helena Medal, was presented to soldiers who had served under Napoleon from 1792 to 1815. The above certificate was awarded to Joseph Cherbonnier and is now in the possession of his descendant, Ben Cherbonnier of Baton Rouge, Louisiana.

Turmoil and Fever

the most prominent exiles, the scholar and educator, Joseph Lakanal. Thank goodness, Guillemin must have thought, the regicide and unfrocked priest was not in New Orleans! But the Lallemand brothers were there often—too often—and in spite of their denials seemed to have a finger or two in the conspiracy.

"If Napoleon should ever come here, I would offer him my home!" Mayor Nicholas Girod had said. Those words obsessed the French Consul. The delta would be an ideal starting point for an expedition. There, in the curves of the Mississippi, in the meanderings of the bayous, screened by the grey draperies of Spanish moss, a frigate could be armed and stocked for a long voyage. The *demi-soldes* and their friends, the pirates, would make up a fearless crew. They could even employ a few *marron* slaves only too glad to buy their freedom at the cost of storms or attacks.

Such an undertaking would be costly. Who would furnish the money? The Creoles? With their large families, uncertain crops, and social obligations, which for them was a duty, it is doubtful they would provide much cash. Nicholas Girod? So many requests had been addressed to him that his fortune had dwindled to the extent that he no longer was able to help Jean Claude Hudry, his Savoy compatriot, an ex-soldier of the Imperial armies, who was now in need. Pierre Caillou? No doubt the ebullient Gascon would deem it an honor to participate in such an enterprise, but there is a difference between treating one's friends to dinners and drinks and equipping a vessel. Moreover, the time was not far off when one of the Bordelais' most frequent guests, Caius Gracchus Fleuriau, would record in his diary a loan made to his too generous host.

Charles Lallemand? Mr. de Feriet ceaselessly complained that his tenant defaulted. Henri Lallemand? Suddenly an idea struck François Guillemin. Henri? No, but rather his wife's uncle and foster father, Stephen Girard, a former cabin boy from Bordeaux, now a Philadelphia millionaire who, according to the rumor, had helped the United States financially during the War of 1812. He did so as much out of gratitude for his new country as out of his hatred of England. This hatred might prompt him to play a trick on Sir Hudson Lowe who, for Anglophobes, was the epitome of villainy. Girard, once shunned by society, was flattered to have become a former king's banker and trusted advisor. He accepted no payment for his services, his only reward being a bust of Napoleon by Canova and the honor of having a Bonaparte come to his Sunday receptions. Joseph and his glittering escort attended the wedding of Henri and Henriette. The young couple was showered with gold.

Why, in the midst of the honeymoon, did the groom leave his bride to rush to New Orleans? Was it to attend to his new uncle's business? Girard had properties in Louisiana. A planter, being unable to pay a sum he owed to Parisian banker Jacques Laffite, had asked for Girard's help, giving in exchange a large section of Ouachita Parish and a 500-ton frigate, *La Superbe*.

La Superbe! Could it be the key to the enigma, the Consul wondered? *"Si non e verro e ben trobato!"* (Let us hope that other appeals will calm down the conspirators' enthusiasm or other events will interfere!)

In the Buisson brothers' minds dreams of heroism and of love must have mingled. The dazzling autumn had cleared away the cruel summer's last traces. The air was as intoxicating as the Louisiana wine made from oranges or wild cherries. Fra Antonio de Sedella, who had become for most Orleanians their beloved Père Antoine, opened his large register at St. Louis Cathedral. With a handwriting as angular as his long face, he certified in Spanish that he had officiated at the marriage ceremony of Frederico Buisson and Isabella Guillotte. Joy and pride filled the prettily attired maid of honor's heart, and Benjamin realized that Sophie was sixteen years old. A ripe age for a young *demoiselle*!

The following Spring the names Buisson and Guillotte again found a place in St. Louis Cathedral's big book. The newly married were Pedro Buisson and Sofia Guillotte. Jacques and Enoul de Livaudais were among the witnesses, which indicates that Bonaparte's ex-lieutenant had been accepted by Creole society. On the eve of the wedding a contract had been made before a notary. The bride was bringing household linen, silverware, and a dowry that was not too large but would provide that minimum of security without which even the most adventurous men, if they come from the Old World, do not feel at ease. The two couples lived in a house on St. Philip Street. Late at night they could hear men shuffling toward Pierre Laffite's blacksmith shop, a few doors distant.

Other *demi-soldes* settled in homes more often poor than luxurious. Sometimes all that they owned was a cabin on the edge of a bayou. No Père Antoine and no official authority was available to legalize their marriages. As pledge of their good faith, bride and groom held hands and jumped over a broom handle held above the ground by two witnesses. Later on, perhaps a pirogue would bring a bearded missionary who would bless the parents and baptize the children. At least, that was the woman's hope. But the veteran was wondering if someday a signal coming across the swamps or along the waterways would not call him to the service of the hero that time and distance were magnifying.

VI

Death Comes to the Emperor

THE MUSÉE WAS LOCATED AT THE CORNER of Chartres and Jefferson streets. The Musée was really a café to which the owners, Messieurs Turpin and Dorfeuille, attracted customers by announcing in the gazettes that for two *escalins* one could see rare insects, reptiles, exotic birds and sea shells. People who went once returned bringing their friends. The reptiles were harmless, the birds not too noisy, the tafia was good and the atmosphere pleasant.

One evening in 1821 the clients (only men, since no respectable woman would have entered a café, even if it was called museum) were listening to Fleury Generelly describe a trip he had taken on a big paddle-wheel boat, the *Maid of Orleans*. During the slow voyage he had made clever little sketches and now he displayed them.

Suddenly a loud voice calling an order interrupted the speaker. Emotion spread across Generelly's sensitive face. Pushing aside his listeners, he rushed to the place from which the call had come. What happened then would have inspired Greuze's brush or Jean Jacques Rousseau's pen during the over-sentimental era of the 18th century. Throwing his arms around the newcomer, Generelly called him "my savior!" Then, with an emphatic gesture, he introduced "Gleize Langdac . . . with-

Death Comes to the Emperor 83

out him, I would not be alive." Everyone in the café wanted to hear about the rescue which could be vouched for by the gray-haired Langdac and the contents of Generelly's little diary.

Fleury was the offspring of a noble Roman family, the Generelly de Rinaldi who, for some obscure reason, had moved to France upon the advice of Cardinal Fleury, Louis XV's state minister. The benefactor's memory prompted the name given to a child born on the last day of 1779. The boy was big enough eleven years later to take part in one of the Federation feasts celebrating the new France. In Lyons, on Place des Terreaux, he joined in singing hymns to virtue and civism while rose petals were thrown from children's be-ribboned baskets. Optimism did not last long. Most Lyonnais were Royalists. When they rebelled against the Convention's commissaries an army was sent to subdue them. They closed the gates of the city and organized a resistance. Fleury, then fourteen years old, was placed as a sentinel at the entrance of the Brotteaux bridge. A barge loaded with projectiles intended to blow up the bridge slowly approached. A man jumped into the Rhone and, ignoring the bullets hitting the water around him, swam to the boat and pulled out the incendiary wick. For the first time Fleury owed his life to a stranger. The second time was soon to come.

After sixty-three days of fierce struggle the Revolutionaries entered the city with the assistance of inside agents. The savage resistance continued but the outnumbered Royalists could not win. Over two hundred prisoners were brought to the Tribunal and condemned to die. With hands tied behind their backs, they were marched toward the Brotteaux plain, the youngest ones in the rear, partly hidden. These children with tied hands, the same hands that had thrown flowers in civic festivals, might have aroused too much sympathy had they been more visible.

Escorted by the firing squad and gendarmes, the condemned men had to cross the Place des Terreaux. They passed in front of the Dames de St. Pierre's convent, now converted into barracks. A few soldiers leaning against the gates looked at the pitiful group approaching. There was a short delay and then the rear-guard appeared with its adolescents. The sudden metallic noise of swords pulled out of scabbards, cords being cut, robust arms seizing the bewildered prisoners and pushing them through the gates—all of these actions were completed in a moment. Gendarmes had not seen, or pretended not to have seen, the last rank's disappearance.

Fleury and about fifteen of his comrades spent the night huddled in a dark cell. What would their fate be? At dawn soldiers entered holding uniforms. When each one of these new recruits had been dressed, in the oversized clothes, a miniature carmagnole was pinned on their lapels as an emblem of their revolutionary faith. Thus, Fleury Théotime Generelly de Rinaldi, to whom a cardinal in heaven extended his protective wings, became a drummer boy in the armies of the First Republic.

He had asked the name of the tall corporal who had saved him. "Gleize," he replied. "They also call me Langdac." The last name probably meant that Gleize came from the Languedoc province. After Fleury had beaten the drum on many battlefields, he received this letter, which he always kept: "I want thee to know, young friend, that the Prefect has approved thy incorporation in the Hussards regiment assembled in this department to serve with the First Consul's reserve at Dijon. I embrace thee.

Death Comes to the Emperor 85

Urbain Jaune, secretary to the Lyons Prefect, 19th of Prairial, year 8 of the Republic."

Generelly asked to be sent to San Domingo. He was made Chief Accountant, an immense task, a few before him had been able to keep a clear record of the expedition's finances. He found time to court and marry a planter's daughter. The Haitian fiasco forced him and his family to seek refuge in the United States. They stopped at Philadelphia but still longed for a sunny climate. Fleury went ahead by boat down the Ohio River, then the Mississippi, taking notes and sketching. On Christmas Eve in 1814, he wrote in his diary: "Arrived in New Orleans at four o'clock in the afternoon and found the city besieged by the English." With his Latin flair for drama, Generelly had landed just in time for the Battle. From then on, his life became closely associated with the lives of other Napoleonic soldiers, the ones who, as himself, came after San Domingo, the ones who, as Gleize and Lavaud, came after Waterloo, and so many others. He shared their small joys, their great hopes, their many sorrows.

The year 1821 was a year of sorrow. During the summer the Frenchmen were made miserable not only by the temperature but also by the news. The first inkling that Napoleon's health was failing came almost three months to the day after his death. When the *Courrier de la Louisiane* and the *Gazette de la Louisiane* were unable to obtain information from arriving vessels, they reprinted articles from New York or Philadelphia. According to a report received in the North, the Emperor's "dissolution was not expected to be distant." This word "dissolution" sounded horrible, but should one trust the press?

Benjamin Buisson may have remembered that the

very week of his landing in New Orleans the *Gazette* had related that a navy captain passing not far from St. Helena had not been able to see the island. Had it sunk into the ocean? It took a few months to ascertain that the captain's error was due to a faulty compass, telescope or his imagination. Perhaps this "dissolution" also was illusive!

Indeed, other papers mentioned that two vessels stopping at St. Helena on April 18 had learned that "Bonaparte was well." Four days later, another comforting piece of news appeared: "Bonaparte was indisposed but not to such a degree as to cause the slightest apprehension for his life." It was followed, however, by a strange remark: "In case of Bonaparte's death at St. Helena his body is to be embalmed and sent to England to satisfy the world that no violence has been inflicted on him." Interest in the prisoner was becoming so acute that on August 10 the *Courrier de la Louisiane*, not having any fresh news for its readers' appetites, covered a whole column with "Napoleon's Maxims and Observations said to be taken from a manuscript found in Las Cases' portfolio."

"Comrades," Pierre Caillou was saying hopefully, "don't forget open house as usual on August 15." August 15, the Emperor's feast day—how impatiently it was awaited! The celebration was commented on for many days, months and sometimes years afterward. Once there had been an unforgettable climax to the fireworks: Napoleon's profile blazing high in the sky above the Mississippi. For the banquet afterward, Bruno Ravel of the *Veau qui Tête* had concocted his most delectable *daube glacée*.

On August 15, 1821, all joy was gone. That very day the newspaper had reported: "There is no longer any hope for Bonaparte." It used the term "Bonaparte" instead of "the Emperor," not out of disrespect, but because it borrowed material from Paris or London where no title was given any longer to the "Usurper."

A disturbing element was added through hints that Napoleon might have been poisoned. His physician, Dr. O'Meara, had refused, so it was said, to take part in such a criminal attempt, but a "more accommodating physician might be found."

Dr. Felix Formento had opened a pharmacy where frequently Frenchmen came to consult him less about their health than about political events. No doubt his opinion was asked about the fact that the loyal Corsican, Dr. Antommarchi, had not been invited to sign the death certificate. The *Courrier de la Louisiane* provoked another explosion when it reprinted an article from the Philadelphia *Aurora*. Reading the autopsy's details, an "Observer," as he signed himself, had noticed a similarity between the conditions of Napoleon's body and the body of a Mr. d'Autrichy from San Domingo. As Generelly, through his marriage, had been acquainted with all the island's aristocratic planters, he could answer the question about d'Autrichy: "That poor fellow, when he heard the revolted Negroes approaching, swallowed a dose of arsenic."

Anyone with a critical mind, however, a Buisson or a Jeannin, may have suspected that the *Aurora* could have been inspired by someone from Joseph Bonaparte's circle. The Count de Survilliers, himself greatly interested in newspaper ventures, as indicated by the fact that he helped to launch the *Courrier des Etats Unis*, might have had a hand in slanting *Aurora*'s articles.

At any rate, the Orleanians' hate for the English was revived. It was directed mostly toward the head of the regime, and the *Courrier* delighted in reproducing a burlesque account of George IV's coronation. When Queen

Caroline died shortly afterward, the same newspaper could not resist quoting this judgment from a Northern publication: "However wicked she was, she could not have been worse than her husband."

It was not until September that a vessel stubbornly and fearlessly flying the tricolor flag brought the official date of the Emperor's death: May 5. In their sorrow the veterans should have thought of the Imperial heir, the chubby and blond King of Rome whom many must have seen in the Tuileries garden a few years before. Strangely enough, when attention was focused on every detail of the great man's life, his son was not mentioned. Schoenbrunn Palace had entombed him more securely than the Capuchins' crypt would do ten years later.

In his Consulate, Guillemin must have sighed with relief. With no more plot to fear, the strict supervision of the ex-soldiers could be relaxed. He may not have been the only one whose anxiety was eased. Sophie and Elizabeth Buisson, Virginie Cuvelier, the young Boutte widow who had become Mrs. Formento and many other wives no doubt thought: no more adventurous schemes, no more wars. But tactfully, as most Louisianians, they enveloped the Frenchmen with their sympathy.

In its issues of October 12 and October 15, the *Courrier de la Louisiane* published an appeal in French and in English: "Persons desirous to contribute to the means of celebrating a funeral service to the memory of Napoleon are invited to meet on the 16th at five o'clock at the Orleans Ballroom. It only appertains to rigid and impartial posterity to fix the place which Napoleon is to occupy among the great men, ancient and modern, but the circumstances of his exile and of his premature death suffice to create the liveliest interest in the minds of all liberal men whatever their nation or sect and to deserve on their part a last tribute to his memory."

This request went straight to the citizens' hearts. But it took two months to prepare the ceremony in the city so fond of pomp and celebration. An insight into the taste for oratory of that time and place is found in a note sent to the *Courrier de la Louisiane* by "Napoleonis Admirator:" "It is with the utmost interest that I read lately . . . that the inhabitants of New Orleans and the Frenchmen who have taken refuge in that city in consequence of the political events in Europe were preparing to celebrate the funeral service of the hero of France in a manner worthy of such a character and with that zeal which shows that the heart alone has dictated the proceeding. However, I see with sorrow that the committee appointed has not immediately chosen one or more orators. . . ." After longer and more flowery sentences, it was suggested that an oratorical contest should take place before carefully selected judges.

While the elaborate preparations were going on, the newspapers kept interest alive. They pointed to Dr. Antommarchi's efforts to obtain the proper clay for a death mask and to Marie Louise's announcement of a complicated but short period of mourning she and her Palma court would observe for her "very serene husband." An anonymous poet sent an acrostic, each letter of the name Napoleon offering a chance to praise this modern Mars, Themis, Pallas, Caesar and Solon, the latter conveniently furnishing the rhyme needed. Another time, a logogriph was printed. No need to wait until the next issue to find the answer. Every reader knew who the greatest captain in the world was. Soldiers suspected the author to be Guillaume Montmain. He should be the one to compose the inscription for the cenotaph!

At that moment all conversation centered upon the cenotaph to be erected in St. Louis Cathedral. Naturally, the architect Buisson and the artistic Generelly were consulted, but the Frenchmen did not accept any suggestion without tossing it around. Often Sophie Buisson or Mme. Generelly had to wait before giving the servant the order to put the tureen of gumbo on the dining table; their husbands, pencil in hand, were discussing the matter. Local organizers were disturbed when a letter printed by the *Gazette de la Louisiane* showed that they had been outdistanced: "Last night, the cannon was fired three times and three times again this morning and twenty-one times during the ceremony. At nine o'clock, the church was filled with persons of both sexes all animated by the same spirit. The service over, each participant went home in the greatest silence. I shall always keep the memory of the feeling of mourning experienced by the inhabitants of this parish."

"St. John the Baptist is not the only parish that worked faster than we," disgruntled Orleanians thought. They were right. "Napoleon is dead!" a pilot going up the Mississippi had roared. Slaves bringing cotton bales to the levee heard him, hustled back to the master's habitation with the news: "Napoleon, *li mouri!*" Choctaws gliding silently on the bayous and the lakes brought the news to the remotest places: "The great *cacique* of the French is dead." In Donaldsonville, Dr. St. Martin and his colleagues from the Russian campaign paused briefly in their endless task of feeding patients quinine and delivering white, black, and amber babies. A former grenadier of the Imperial Guard, now head of a general merchandise store, stood and saluted. The tidings reached a herdsman from Savoy who, when he was nineteen, was said to have raised a cannon on his powerful shoulders to greet Bonaparte crossing the Alps. Bells tolled everywhere.

In New Orleans, at last, plans were taking a concrete

form. At the top of high ladders in St. Louis Cathedral Negroes cleaned the chandeliers; in the sacristy sextons polished and repolished the silver knob of the long cane that rythmically would strike the flagstones during the procession. In a nearby barn, two Italian artists were building the cenotaph and chasing away brown eyes peering through cracks in the walls. Passers-by slowed down to hear the hymns filtering out of the Orleans Theater. John Davis, the impresario formerly from the West Indies, was conducting the rehearsal of a cantata composed especially for the occasion by the beloved music teacher, Cheret.

On the morning of December 19 the mourners assembled at the Charity Lodge on Rampart Street. For this occasion several of the old uniforms had been taken out of the goatskin-covered trunks, but most of the men were wearing the navy blue of the Louisiana Legion on which they had pinned their medals. Benjamin Buisson was at their head. When the marchers turned into Orleans Street the *banquettes* were packed with a mass of onlookers. How strange was that silence compared to the usually noisy exuberance of a New Orleans crowd. Street merchants had stopped calling their wares, servants moved with muffled steps and shopkeepers standing on the thresholds of their closed stores were waiting to take their places in the cortege. Creole ladies on their balconies, fans in hand whatever the season, remained motionless.

The ex-soldiers were marching, erect, proud, sad, each one searching his past for the last time he had seen his Emperor. They were all there, even Garrigues de Flaugeac, who called himself "an adoptive son of the Union," had come from Opelousas; even Humbert who, sober on that day, forgot his rancor to honor adorable Pauline's brother. Present were Lefebvre-Desnouettes, who in the softness of this December morning thought of other harsh winters; the disfigured Rigaud, more silent than ever; the aloof Charles Lallemand; and the *Grande Armée*'s surgeons, Formento, Dubourg, Doussan, Dufour, Monnot, St. Martin, and Jeannin who, like Buisson, had been one of Bonaparte's "golden eggs"; Montmain the songwriter; Montiasse the swordmaster and many more obscure veterans. Bells were tolling. The mourners entered the Cathedral at the sound of Cheret's funeral march. For all those who had ever heard a *Dies Irae* under the vaults of a Gothic church, the organ must have sounded weak indeed, but for once the Frenchmen did not think of criticizing. Moved by the atmosphere of sympathy, a newly arrived Parisian, Caius Gracchus Fleuriau, mentioned in his diary "that imposing tableau worthy of its subject."

After the mayor, Count de Roffignac from Southern France, the dignitaries, the mixed group of free-masons and the ex-soldiers had taken their seats, the public climbed to the gallery. From there they looked down upon the huge catafalque, the trophies, the tricolor banners, the twenty-four silver candlesticks and the tripods holding burning incense. Only from below, however, could one see the inscription "Religion and Fine Arts weeping and throwing flowers on the tomb of Napoleon the Great," and on four panels, in Latin and in French, praises of the Emperor and harsh criticism of Albion.

The mass began. A tall monk slightly bent by age was at the altar. His thrown-back hood revealed an angular face made longer by a pointed beard. Some of the people may have wondered how Fra Antonio de Sedella could offer the Holy Sacrifice for a sovereign who, in the catechism taught to Spanish children, had been identified with Satan. But this padre who had held in check his bishop's power—this proud, stubborn, bellicose padre—could understand Napoleon. Calmed by age, he was now the good pastor who gave dragees and picayunes to urchins. His two acolytes had fought mud and waves for hours in order to attend this service, one coming from St. John the Baptist, the other from Terre aux Boeufs.

Mass was over. The three priests sat in the sanctuary and a layman climbed the steps to the pulpit. Everyone recognized Judge Jean François Canonge, exalted Master of Charity Lodge, head of Louisiana masons and a well-known writer. The next day, the *Gazette de la Louisiane* bluntly reported that no one had heard anything he said. The *Courrier,* more tactful, wrote, "He (Canonge) recited a piece of verses. . . . We regret that he did not on the tomb of the great man strew flowers that he opened himself." The implication was that he was not the author of the poem.

While the bells tolled again, people scattered. Hushed voices grew louder.

"Do you know what the prize will be for tomorrow's lottery? A picture of St. Helena tomb!"

"Will *he* always remain there?"

"Have you read in the *Gazette* that letter from Dr. Antommarchi expressing the desire that the Emperor's body be returned to Paris?"

"What the English hold, they keep."

"Elmire, my child, hurry up. Mr. Audubon is waiting to give you your drawing lesson."

"Wouldn't he be happier watching his birds?"

Colored women were offering dark spice cakes from their baskets. *"Estomacs mulâtres*! Pralines! Pralines!" Soot-covered from his slippers to his high hat, a broom on his shoulder, a chimney sweep passed chanting: *"Ramoner de ci de là, la cheminée du haut en bas!"* (Clean the chimney, here and there, from top to bottom.) Life had started again. The Frenchmen alone did not judge it proper to resume their daily occupations. In small groups they gathered once more to speak about their favorite subject, but they realized that the youthful, adventurous, hopeful part of their lives was over. Yet, the magnifying of a man into a superman had only begun; the Napoleonic legend would soar even higher in Louisiana.

VII

Taps and Gun Salutes

THE *Courrier de la Louisiane* published Napoleon's testament. Orleanians read that the Emperor had remembered with gratitude some of the exiles who had been in their midst. They experienced pride and regret—pride for having played hosts to such important persons, regret for not having done even more for them. Where were they now?

Poor General Rigaud had died. Perhaps the Imperial legacy would go to his son, Narcisse Pericles (who, in spite of his high-sounding name, was clerking in a store), or to his daughter Marie, now tutoring the children of a North Louisiana planter.

Charles Lallemand certainly could find some use for the 100,000 francs bequeathed to him, but what he would do with the money was guesswork. Lallemand, who had boasted of his desire to cultivate the rich Louisiana soil, had left his house down the Mississippi without paying his debts, and the little farm had fallen into the hands of his creditors. Why had all his interest in the South left him after the Emperor's death? Through the newspapers it was learned that the restless general was traveling from one continent to another. He went to Brussels, then back to New York where he opened a school. It would take ten years and the advent in France of the more liberal regime of Louis Philippe I for him to be reinstated in the army and have his title of Peer restored to him.

Henri's fate was different. He remained for a while in New Orleans writing an artillery treatise. In 1823, shortly after his wife in Philadelphia had given him a daughter, he returned to her. He was already quite ill. In spite of Stephen Girard's care, or perhaps because of the home-made remedies, which the eccentric millionaire preferred to any doctor's advice, he died. Eight years later, Girard joined him in the same tomb after writing a will leaving a legacy to New Orleans. Why such a vivid interest in the Southern port? Was it because of what he had heard about the city's Bonapartist fervor?

General Lefebvre-Desnouettes, thanks to his wife's tireless efforts and the intercession of banker Jacques Lafitte and other influential relatives and friends, received the much coveted authorization to return to France, but not to Paris. He immediately sailed for Europe. A few months later readers of the gazettes in the Chartres Street's *cabinet de lecture* were shocked. The vessel carrying Lefebvre-Desnouettes had crashed on rocks in view of the Irish coast. Pursued by misfortune, the officer drowned a few feet from rescuers who were hampered by furious waves. "Why was he traveling on the *Albion*?" wondered some Frenchmen, for whom that name was anathema.

Another general whose personality was even more familiar to the Orleanians also disappeared from the scene in 1823. Once a month, passersby on Royal or Toulouse Streets would stare at a huge man in military garb complete with tarnished epaulettes, greenish gold braid and tattered plumed hat on unkempt gray hair. On that day, Jean Joseph Amable Humbert would march to the

French Consulate to receive his pension. The amount doled out was small. Luckily there were still a few youngsters who would go to his lodging on Casa Calvo Street near Elysian Fields. Under the pretense of being coached in mathematics, they would listen breathlessly to tales of conquests of all sorts. The few *piastres* they discreetly left as fees helped the old officer without hurting his pride.

After the General's sojourn in the Calaboose in 1820, New Orleans society had shunned him. On the other hand, gamblers, smugglers and the dregs of a large port welcomed him. One night he was the guest of honor at a banquet tendered to him by pirates. The master of ceremonies, a Baratarian wearing the traditional greasy kerchief and a single gold earring, stood and offered a toast to Humbert. Carried away by wine and enthusiasm, he launched into a dramatic recital of the General's exploits: Landau . . . Vendée . . . Ireland . . . San Domingo . . . the Battle. . . . Suddenly, he was interrupted. Humbert's fist violently hammered the table. "And to think that I am ending such a career among the brigands you are!" His face purple with anger, his shoulders shaken with sobs, he staggered toward the door.

The next day the whole city was abuzz over the incident. "Do you think that he was drunk?" Frenchmen asked each other. "Perhaps not. Perhaps his conscience spoke. Who knows?" In the sequel to that incident, pride, shame or the regret of having offended his only friends kept Humbert more isolated. Little was written about him in the local newspapers when he died in early January. People returning New Year's calls may have passed that meager funeral procession conducted by Père Antoine, more bent and angular than ever. No record shows that the Louisiana Legion rallied to the old soldier's grave.

About that time Pierre Laffite's blacksmith shop was closed and he and his brother disappeared. After the affair in which the Creole lady's jewels were found in the loot brought from Grande Terre, hostile looks followed Jean and Pierre when they passed on the streets. They decided they would feel more at ease in the Red Fort. But the Government, determined to stop piracy, sent a small fleet to dislodge them. It was rumored that Jean gave his men the order never to shoot back at any vessel flying the Stars and Stripes.

Much later, *De Bow's Review* published a dramatic account of Jean's last battle: "Above the tumult Laffite's firm voice was heard, his arm dripping with blood was still holding a broken blade. . . ." After having quoted the buccaneer's last words, the narrator prudently added: "There are some who think that he is still alive as no authentic story of his death has even been printed." Thus, the great chief of the Gulf's buccaneers preserved the aura of mystery which gave heroic proportions to all the outlaws of the romantic period.

The disappearance of the Laffites, Lallemands, Lefebvre-Desnouettes, Humbert and even the silent Rigaud must have been felt by the ex-soldiers. It added to the effect already created by the Emperor's death. A curtain had been drawn over a time of restlessness. Now they would accept a more disciplined line of conduct. Even the privateer Dominique You was growing tame. He and his former partner in adventures, Simon Laignel, abandoned their Caribbean expeditions and opened a *Jardin de Plaisance* (small amusement park) on an islet between two arms of the Mississippi. Barges brought merry groups to the park. A collation was served and the guests were invited to help themselves to the peaches, figs, grapes and oranges of the orchard. Then there was dancing to the sound of violins and clarinets. The *Jardin de Plaisance* was advertised widely in the newspapers. No doubt among its customers were many exiles. Should they still be called exiles?

Most of them had already crossed this imaginary frontier that uprooted people build around themselves. First, it was through the long ocean voyage when they had parted from their country. Later, it would be through omissions. Buisson and his comrades probably did not scan the column announcing the arrival of boats coming from Europe before reading local news. They did not dash to the levee to question landing travelers. Their sympathy for a homesick newcomer was less spontaneous. Buisson even mixed into Louisiana politics, taking part in elections since a non-citizen apparently had the right to vote, at least at some level. After several years in this softer climate his bearing was less military, his speech less abrupt. He was probably saying *banquette* for sidewalk and *char* for carriage. Yet he remained transfixed with emotion when he heard the never-forgotten *Marseillaise*.

Buisson must have been touched when during a ceremony he became the recipient of the Legion Flag. *"Honneur, patrie, discipline, valeur"* were embroidered in gold on a deep azure silk. On the other side the same words were repeated in English. In the center was an eagle surrounded by stars. Of course, it was the American eagle, but it reminded the ex-soldiers of the golden eagles they had followed through European battlefields. It must have sounded strange for Captain Buisson to hear his voice pronouncing in English the pledge of allegiance in front of the Governor. "I swear to Your Excellency in my name and in my comrades' names to preserve this flag from any stain and if ever a call to arms be heard, the Orleans Battalion would never come back without having covered this standard with laurels." The accent was still French and the words somewhat pompous, but it was typical of the time and place.

"This country has been good to you," Sophie might have said to her husband. The country had been good to him, and he appreciated that feeling of solidarity between Creoles and Frenchmen. Not that they did not sometimes experience slight difficulties, but difficulties occur in the best of households.

For the ex-Napoleonic soldiers Louisiana's feast days had become their own. Each year the Legion commemorated the Battle of January 8. A procession made up of all the State and City dignitaries marched to the Cathedral where the flag was blessed while the organ played a *Te Deum*. On the Place d'Armes cannoneers fired gun salutes to punctuate different moments of the religious service taking place inside. Then all the men gathered in the best hotel for a *"jovial banquette,"* as the gazettes would say the next day. Numerous toasts were drunk. Once General and Senator Garrigues de Flaugeac came from Opelousas to celebrate the famous 1815 anniversary. With such a master of ceremonies no one could be forgotten, and the newspapers reported sixteen toasts. In the midst of the libations someone remembered that a Presidential election was going to take place that year and a drink to the future President was proposed: "May he be a man who knows that the State of Louisiana exists!" After this somewhat sarcastic wish there was a silence. Then the Frenchmen whispered to each other and made a sign to their Captain. Benjamin stood up and with a grave voice proclaimed: "To the Emperor Napoleon, great in the history of the world, great in adversity!" Later on, he wrote a report about the day's events. His artillerymen had fired their guns 225 times in five minutes, showing that they had reached the *"sommet de l'instruction."* To reward them, this "assemblage of brothers" was invited to the Orleans Theater to attend a gala presided over by the Mayor, Count de Roffignac. It was a farewell occasion as Roffignac had decided to go back to his chateau at his native Dordogne.

Each year, on St. Barbe's feast day, cannoneers marched through the city, flowers at the mouths of the guns, bands playing as in every French town. On July 4th, the Legionaries wore their white uniforms. When the parade was over, they went to picnic on the levee where year after year they noticed fewer sailboats, more paddleboats and quite a few steamboats. With demi-johns of good wine they remained until swarms of mosquitoes chased them away, and they went home singing at the top of their husky voices the verses the local poet Tullius de St. Céran had composed in honor of Benjamin Buisson's regiment: "Who gathers the most beautiful laurels? The Artilleryman, The Artilleryman!"

The chief himself must have hummed those words when his friend Jeannin told him that a Frenchman had arrived whose name was familiar to the two former Polytechniciens: "Lakanal? You don't mean the Joseph Lakanal of the Paris Institute?" "Himself."

It is only through hearsay that men of Jeannin's or Buisson's age knew about the early part of Lakanal's peripatetic career. The French Revolution had opened new doors to this studious Southerner who until then had been guided and encouraged by the village priest, his instructor, to become a member of the clergy. He threw himself into politics, forgot about his cassock and voted death for Louis XVI. As a reward he was appointed Director of the Public Education Committee in charge of founding the Ecole Normale Supérieure for higher education and opening secondary Central Schools. He also had a hand in the creation of the Ecole Polytechnique and became one of the first members of the Institute, made up of the French Academy plus other scholarly groups.

The Imperial Regime was not too profitable for the opportunistic Lakanal. Bonaparte distrusted ideologists and turncoats. To find himself an *économe*, an accountant, in a Lycée, and later an Inspector of Weights and Measures, was a disgrace for someone who had aimed so high. Yet Napoleon's fall hurt Lakanal still more. The former regicide did not wait to see his name on a proscription list. He sailed away and arrived at Philadelphia in time to be one of the first exiles to render homage to Count de Survillier. He put his personal seal on the plan of the Napoleonic Confederation. While the French and Spanish ambassadors who had an inkling of the plot fretted and appealed to President Monroe, Lakanal, cautious as usual, left for a Kentucky farm where he could be forgotten for the time being.

He had been there for a few years when he received a letter from the Board of the Orleans College in Louisiana. Buisson and Jeannin must have been familiar with this establishment since it sheltered another ex-artillery lieutenant, Pierre Guillot, who had become a mathematics professor. A shelter it was, nothing more. The institution was rapidly declining. To the few paying students a handful of poor children uncharitably called *élèves de charité* (charity pupils) had been added. Among the faculty were cultured but eccentric San Domingans among whom Pierre Guillot felt lost. "If at least I could be sure to be paid at the end of the month," he sighed. Financial problems were pressing. A tax on gambling houses, however numerous they were, and on popular lotteries never brought enough to remedy the deficit. A few Creoles promised funds, but in order to obtain more it would be necessary to enhance the college's prestige. Why not import a well-known European educator? No need to waste months corresponding across the ocean. Monsieur Lakanal of the Institut de France was in Kentucky. Nobody could have been happier with the offer than Monsieur Lakanal.

In spite of April showers which almost turned Rampart Street into a swamp, most of New Orleans attended the investiture of Orleans College's new president. A heavy-set man with dark hair, Lakanal did not look old in spite of his sixty or more years. He spoke with a strong, solemn voice. First, the public listened with a respectful curiosity, then with respect only, then with boredom. Weighing each word, the orator reviewed his long career, omitting none of his titles. From time to time, he pointed to a pile of references and picked up a flattering sentence. Lafayette had praised him, as had Geoffroy de St. Hilaire, and also... and also... The listeners whose attention had strayed could refresh their memories the next day as the inaugural speech was printed in its entirety by the local press.

For many weeks to follow Lakanal made the news, but not always in the same complimentary way. He was bringing to the revival of the college the same energy he formerly had used for larger enterprises. He took as models the Central Schools, now called Lycées. In contrast to religious institutions, the emphasis was not on the humanities but on sciences and practical notions useful in everyday life. Laboratories would be well equipped. In workshops adolescents following in the steps of Jean Jacques Rousseau's Emile would carve wood and build furniture. There would also be a botanical garden where the students, loyal disciples of Buffon, would learn to appreciate nature. Not only should they develop their minds and their skills, but they should become aware of their country's needs. Thus a course could teach young Louisianians constantly under the threat of Mississippi floods "the methods of ancient and modern peoples, especially the Dutch who always had to protect themselves against the invasion of sea and rivers."

Buisson, Jeannin and Pierre Guillot, among others, must have watched those efforts with interest and pride. No doubt success would be reached. The number of pupils soon jumped from seven to eighty. In the grandiloquent reports Lakanal sent to Parisian colleagues no one could have suspected the small size of the Collège d'Orléans. Local newspapers proudly mentioned that President Lakanal was receiving demands of admission from as far as Kentucky. It was good news for Creole parents who often sent their sons to Transylvania University in Kentucky because they had not found an institution of equal value in the Deep South.

Would Lakanal continue his ascent? Charles Cuvelier, who had encountered difficulties in organizing boys' schools, was pessimistic. Readers of the *Courrier de la Louisiane* became irritated by the impression Lakanal conveyed that his presence in New Orleans would be the salvation of its youth. In July, 1823, fourteen months after his investiture, President Lakanal offered his resignation. It was immediately accepted.

Questions were on every lip. Had the city founded by a Bourbon revolted against the importance conferred upon a regicide? Did Creole mothers, who went to church while their husbands met at the Free Masonic Lodge, dislike having their children entrusted to an unfrocked priest? Yet that unsavory past must have been overlooked when he was invited.

Taps and Gun Salutes

Three months after the well-attended investiture, the planter de Fériet, who might have become bitter through his dealings with Charles Lallemand, wrote his sister that Lakanal was boring everybody "with his bombastic language and his boasting." Less than a year later, he announced to this same sister, with what amounted to a sigh of relief, that New Orleans was about to get rid of this *impitoyable bavard* (relentless chatterbox).

Perhaps it was to assume an air of importance that "citizen Lakanal" visited sugar refineries with the object of buying them for "his friend, Count de Survilliers, ex-King of Spain." Was jealousy inspiring de Fériet's comments? At that time, he was pressuring the millionaire de Marigny to acquire Mortfontaine, a property Joseph Bonaparte still owned in France. The Creole gentleman and the college president were more or less on the same hunting grounds.

Lakanal's desires for reform had extended beyond academic fields. Having been invited to join the Société Médicale, he urged the acquisition of a machine to purify the air. This project was probably discussed in Dr. Formento's pharmacy. He and Dr. Honoré Doussan of Montpellier, Dufour and other physicians must have been reminded of well-intentioned Eudes de Gentilly's similar offer and subsequent downfall. Lakanal's refusal to declare that someday he would become an American citizen had hurt his position. His was not the only such case, however.

In the fall of 1820 when more and more French refugees were arriving by way of Alabama or Texas, Louisiana was in the midst of a gubernatorial campaign. Orleanians seemingly had agreed not to confer any political power on anyone born on the other side of the ocean. Following suit, the Louisiana Legion revolted against the choice of a Frenchman as commander, and the mortified Cuvelier had to withdraw his candidacy temporarily. However, Pierre Benjamin Buisson and some of the former *demi-soldes* remained French, yet were accepted as leaders. It could be said that for sensitive Orleanians naturalization meant less a legal process than an attitude. Lakanal, pompous, pedantic, sarcastic and domineering, never succeeded in being accepted by local citizens.

Upon leaving New Orleans Lakanal settled on a small estate outside Mobile on the Gulf shore. There had been a Madame Lakanal, although she did not cut a large figure in society. The couple had a daughter who married Lucien Charvet, a young man who had spent a year at the Ecole Polytechnique before Louis XVIII had the time to dismiss the cadets chosen by the Imperial regime. After Lakanal's departure, Lucien Charvet and Pierre Guillot kept their positions until political and financial difficulties obliged the institution to close its gates. When it happened the former president must have flashed his sardonic smile: "So, those Creoles had pretended they could do without me!" When in 1837 he returned to France, the Louisiana episode must have appeared as one short dark period in a very long career.

Joseph Lakanal's sojourn in New Orleans had not been favorable to the French element of the city because of the unfortunate human tendency to hold a whole group responsible for the faults of one individual. But this period of disfavor was short, as was reflected in newspaper accounts of Orleanians' excitement at the approaching visit of another famous Frenchman who was including them in his triumphal tour of the United States. Sixty-eight years old, but still erect, elegant, smiling and thirsty for fame, the Marquis de Lafayette, accompanied by his son, George Washington de Lafayette, arrived on the *Natchez,* a packet boat sent to Mobile to meet him.

A few Bonapartists may have remembered that Lafayette and Napoleon had little regard for each other, but why throw stones in clear water? Artillerymen had been posted on a bend of the Mississippi to give a signal of the arrival of the *Natchez.* At the Place d'Armes gun salutes answered. For five days, in spite of spring showers drenching the crowd, citizens cheered the old soldier as he gamely went from reception to reception, from banquet to ball. With his usual gentle dignity he accepted a present of land from Louisiana. Enthusiasm never cooled and when Lafayette left, his carriage was escorted by an endless procession in which ninety Cherokees in their best array took part. Naturally, the Legion marched at the head. But on that spring day in 1825 it was not commanded by Benjamin Buisson. Other duties or other plans had called him out of the city.

VIII

Call from the Good Earth

"How is the soil over there?"

"Good! You just have to scratch it and everything grows. Three or four crops a year, that is not unusual."

"Four crops a year? But what about help?"

"As much as you want and cheap." A hand pointed toward a group of dark workers.

Such questions and answers were exchanged between planters or foremen supervising the unloading of cotton bales on the wharf and French newcomers who had been reared on farms or in villages and who already felt uncomfortable in a city. For former Alabama or Texas colonists, the memories they kept were not encouraging. However, they realized that on the banks of the Tombigbee or of the Trinity they had been like a shipwrecked crew on a deserted island. Here, west of New Orleans along Bayou Lafourche, it would be different; they would find guides and helping hands among people who spoke their own language and boasted of their happy life in their *paroisse* (parish).*

Paroisse brought to mind the vision of a steeple overlooking a public square where one danced on Sundays

---

* In Louisiana an administrative division, equivalent to a county.

and, for the *Méridionaux* (Southerners), a bowling alley under the shady trees of their esplanade where young girls strolled by. The planters' daughters who often came to do their shopping were not so different from the Bordelaises or the Toulousaines. A few had blue eyes, revealing their Norman origin, but brunettes and blondes spoke French and often stole glances toward the young men of military bearing loitering on the wharves. "How is the soil over there?" was a frequent question. The answer was always encouraging. There was much land to be cultivated and many daughters in need of husbands.

All the names of the exiles who scattered throughout Louisiana have not been recorded, but some of them are still remembered, either because of their descendants' justifiable pride or because of some unusual trait or adventure. For example, there was Louis Gustave Bezou who, being a Breton, was attracted by the sea. As a lieutenant in the Imperial Navy, he fought at Aboukir and at Trafalgar. During his San Domingo stay he married Emilie de Montagnac. After they took refuge in Louisiana he became an *économe* (accountant) on a plantation in Iberville Parish. He died as early as 1825 but left a large and well-known descendance.

Another seaman, Tasset, settled where the salty breezes from the Gulf could reach him. There was Prosper Foy, one of those exuberant men from Bordeaux who had weathered the Antilles expedition. He gathered around him a bunch of fiery Bonapartists. Often, writing in their behalf, he sent a number of letters and songs *a la Bérenger* to the gazettes.

It seems ironic that the flat Bayou Lafourche section could attract Pierre Charlet from the mountainous Grenoble. Yet, he made his home at Belle Alliance. No doubt he frequently found an excuse to leave the care of his herds and ride toward the general store at the junction of two streams. For the Frenchmen of this region it was the counterpart of the Tremoulet or the Cafe Turpin. Travelers landing from barges listened over endless cups of inky coffee. Indians bringing furs and pickaninnies sucking pieces of sugarcane stared at those men in whose boisterous speech a single word repeatedly was heard: Napoleon.

The little community that sprang up around the general store became known as Napoleonville. A church was built and, naturally, named St. Napoleon's after a Greek martyr of the first century conveniently dug out of obscurity. It was under this name that the church was consecrated in 1872 by Archbishop Napoleon Joseph Perché, of Angers, France. When a new church was erected at the beginning of the 20th century, however, St. Napoleon was demoted in favor of St. Ann, who received Archbishop Blenk's blessing in 1909.

When fevers struck it was no longer necessary to turn to an Indian medicine man or an old mammy, although they still remained popular. Now there were real doctors. François Prévost, a graduate of Paris Medical School and a refugee of the West Indies campaign, had attracted around him younger colleagues: Gourrier, St. Martin and Monnot, all from the *Grande Armée*. Joseph St. Martin, born in Chambery, Savoy, in 1792, was an assistant surgeon at the age of twenty. In the aftermath of Waterloo, he came to the United States and practiced medicine at Donaldsonville near the Mississippi River. He married a New Orleans girl, Emilie Constance Dumond.

Charles Monnot had carefully preserved a letter signed by the commandant of the fortified city of Besançon stating the services he had rendered during the 1814 campaign "while the besieged city was crowded with an extraordinary number of sick." But what earned Monnot even more prestige was the fact that Jean Laffite, who had met him during the tragic Galveston hurricane, had vainly tried to attach him to his staff. Several times pirates had been seen lying in ambush behind the physician's house waiting to kidnap him. Napoleonville citizens would have risked a war with the buccaneers rather than lose their good doctor.

He became a still more valuable member of the community when he married a thirteen-year-old Acadian girl named Josephine Bourgeois. He initiated her in the art of handling mortar and pestle. "Quick, Josephine," he would tell her. "We need more quinine. There are five with fever at the Charlet's and six at the Boudreauxs'." Josephine could assist in nursing the Boudreauxs and the Charlets, the Arceneauxs and the Broussards.

The Acadians were sturdy people. Clinging to their Roman Catholic faith and their French language, they were banished from Nova Scotia by the British at the end of the 18th century. Many families became separated when they moved. Many of them in the course of their wanderings, pathetically depicted in Longfellow's *Evangeline*, took refuge in the South. They brought with them their culture and traditions.

The women, wearing their wide skirts, tight bodices, snow-white fichus, bonnets and aprons, dyed and wove the cotton of their fields while children braided sharp palmetto leaves into large sun hats. They sang the same tunes their cousins were still singing at Rouen or Quebec: "*Alouette, gentille alouette...*" Many Napoleonic exiles found among these girls strong and cheerful helpmates.

There were other French elements to be encountered in the parishes, especially at the former military outposts where French people and influence had lingered. The de la Houssayes, the Oliviers de Vezin, the de Clouets, the d'Hauterives, the Van Voorhies who, in spite of their Dutch name had been adopted by the clan, the Blancs d'Erneville and the Fuzeliers de la Claire, the latter being descendants of the first Attakapas post commander, all formed an elegant nucleus. They dressed well, danced minuets and invited itinerant troops of actors to perform in the village of St. Martin, which boasted of being a *Petit Paris.*

It is not surprising that such communities attracted emigrants. Jean Julien Rousseau and Benoit Bayard met there, each proud of his service with Napoleon. Rousseau was fond of explaining how he had taken care of the Emperor's slight wound at Wagram. For his reward, he had been offered a sword which would be the most precious legacy of his children and their grandchildren. Bayard had done even more for Napoleon, or so he claimed. He said he had saved Napoleon's life by pulling out the wick of the cannon aimed at the Emperor. As a result, he had been given the title of Baron, which he would pass on to his descendants. Whenever anyone objected that democratic Americans did not recognize titles, Bayard replied that no law could forbid him to have his sons baptized "Hyppolite and Alfred *Baron* Bayard," and their names were so recorded on their tombstones.

The Attakapas post had a strong rival in the Opelousas post. The latter had been established by Louis XIV more than a century and a half earlier. At the end of their terms of service some of the officers, rather than return to France and live in the shadow of their eldest brothers, had chosen to remain in the New World. One could have more servants here than his father had in his chateau. Their skin was a different color, but who cared? The evergreen oaks, the pecan trees and the magnolias offered more beautiful foliage than the park at Versailles. Jean Jacques Rousseau had spoken the truth: a return to nature was good. The de Tillys, the de la Morandières, the de Blieux and at least ten others did not return to Europe. It is among their descendants that one of the most remarkable of all Napoleonic exiles lived and died.

In 1780, in a chateau overlooking the Lot River in Southern France, Louis Joseph Paul Antoine Garrigues de Flaugeac was born. His father, a former bodyguard at the court of Louis XVI, dreamed of a military career for his son, but before the child had reached the required age to enter the Vendome cavalry school the Revolution closed it. The de Flaugeac residence, luckily, was protected from violence by its isolation and loyal servants. There the adolescent studied mathematics with his father's help. When he was seventeen, he begged to be allowed to serve in Bonaparte's army. Not far from the chateau was an inn owned by the Murat family. If a de Flaugeac had stopped there before the Revolution, it would have been to have the son take care of his horse. Times had changed. General Joachim Murat, visiting his parents' home while on leave, was flattered now to see one of his distant neighbors soliciting his advice.

Young de Flaugeac was blessed with a splendid physique and pleasing manners. Murat promised to call him to his staff as soon as he took command of the reserve army assembled by the First Consul. A few months later, when Garrigues arrived at the Headquarters, he was doubly welcome since he brought the glamorous Murat news of the birth of his first son, Achille. As a subaltern in the Dragoons corps, de Flaugeac took part in the Italian campaign, which was crowned by the Marengo victory.

His spirit of adventure then led him to ask to join the San Domingo expedition. His request was granted. When he reached Cap François, carrying a letter of recommendation for Marshal Leclerc, the latter was dying. General Clausel assumed his protection and appointed him to an artillery regiment. Neither yellow fever nor a deep wound were enough to stop the young giant. For his courage and boldness in battles he was awarded the gold epaulettes, insigna of the rank of officer. Soon afterward, he was captured by a British landing force and sent to a Cuban jail, where his word of honor not to escape kept him there more securely than walls or chains could have. A truce was declared, followed by an amnesty, and prisoners were granted permission to sail home. One of the vessels carrying the freed prisoners was lost at sea. Men on a raft were picked up by a merchant ship heading toward New Orleans.

Big Louis Fontenot was on the levee watching the unloading of his barges. Among the longshoremen of all colors he noticed three handsome youths in tattered clothes. He called to them. They introduced themselves: Van Hill, De Baillon, Garrigues de Flaugeac.

"You must not have done this kind of work very long?"

They laughed. It was their first day, they told him, but they would do anything to repay the crew who had saved their lives.

Fontenot liked their answer. "And what are you going to do next?"

They shrugged; the future did not frighten them.

"Why not come to the Opelousas? There are opportunities there and real gentlemen from your own country."

The offer was accepted.

A boat carried them up the Mississippi River, then on a bayou, then on the picturesque Atchafalaya River,

Call from the Good Earth

then on another bayou. After several days of gliding between low banks edged with reeds out of which egrets and flamingoes sometimes flew up, they stopped in front of barges crammed with cotton bales. "Where are we?" the travelers asked. "At Church Landing, near the Post of the Opelousas, my home!" Big Louis cheerfully exclaimed.

The time was January, 1805. In September of the same year, Marie Louise Fontenot, age fourteen, had made a cross as her signature on her wedding certificate. She was marrying in St. Landry parish the handsomest of the three Frenchmen, Garrigues de Flaugeac. Marie Louise had two sisters and soon Opelousians were invited to two other wedding feasts. The one-time military outpost was richer by three energetic citizens and Big Louis had acquired three good sons-in-law: de Flaugeac, de Baillon, and Van Hill, the latter referred to by Bayou Courtableau's inhabitants as *Monsieur Vanille*.

Things did not always run smoothly at the Opelousas. Descendants of post commanders pretended to exercise authority. One of them took it upon himself to grant divorces in spite of missionaries' indignation. There were squabbles between colonists. One said he had received his land from a Spanish Governor. Unfortunately, it overlapped a property whose deed, bearing a *fleur de lys* seal, had been granted to a neighbor. Pioneers in the shelter of a virgin forest or isolated by a swamp sometimes squatted on estates that already had claimants. If only there was someone who knew how to survey, someone whose honesty was beyond reproach, someone patient enough to listen to arguments and courageous enough not to fear reprisals!

"Why not my eldest son-in-law?" Fontenot suggested.

Garrigues de Flaugeac was more than a surveyor. He was a respected advisor, the judge chosen by the community. When in 1812 the Louisiana territory became a state, the ex-lieutenant of the dragoons was elected one of its first senators. That rank of lieutenant, anyway, belonged to a distant past. Garrigues was too dynamic a power in the Legion not to have reached in a few strides the title of brigadier general.

It was December, 1814. Gliding along Bayou Courtableau, a messenger brought the startling news that New Orleans was expecting an imminent landing by British troops. Hastily, de Flaugeac put on his Legion uniform, said goodbye to his wife, little daughters Celeste and Claire and his new-born son, Adolphe, and left on the first boat paddling toward the Delta. Later, when the Chalmette battle had been won, without waiting to receive General Jackson's compliments, this hero of Battery Five returned to his family, his plantation, and his duties as a just and benevolent lord.

Big Louis Fontenot had attracted him to the Opelousas. In turn, Garrigues de Flaugeac probably was the guiding hand which some ten years later attracted a new group of Napoleonic exiles.

What a relief for Charles Genin after more than a decade spent on English pontoons to find himself on firm soil—and what a soil!—under the evergreen trees of St. Landry Parish. Yet, he had brought from his long prison life something besides bitter memories.

He had brought a parchment on which another prisoner patiently had painted vignettes around a statement to the effect that Charles François Genin, ex-cannoneer of the Marines, was an accomplished officer and a man of honor to whom all Frenchmen owed assistance in case of need. All his comrades had signed, some illegibly, others with big round childish letters. Still more useful than the diploma on which a green-robed goddess with puffed cheeks blew a bugle was the fact that during his years of captivity Genin had learned a trade. He was now a goldsmith. One of the first rings he made was for his own fiancée Marguerite, an orphan who had been raised by the de la Morandière after the death of her father, the Marchese Gradenico, who for some obscure reason had fled his Venetian palace and taken refuge at the Opelousas.

Another ring was selected in Genin's shop after long talks, probably less about the present than the past. The ring was being purchased by Pierre Gabriel Wartelle. A picture remains showing the young man as thin and elegant, with an impudent nose and tousled blond hair. He looked very much like a Parisian of the Romantic group in spite of his Flemish name. A former cadet of the Fontainebleau Military School, he distinguished himself in the course of several campaigns and was promised the Legion of Honor. Less fortunate than Benjamin Buisson, he did not receive the diploma awarding it. The Empire had collapsed and the new regime ignored promises made by its predecessor. Dissatisfied and restless, Wartelle left for America.

He decided to build himself a home in a shady, picturesque nook of Washington Parish in Louisiana. While the house was being built, he lived with his bride in a plain cabin near the piles of cypress beams and bricks. Some of the lumber was promptly used to make shelves along the hall. Wartelle must have been an avid reader. The works of Corneille, Racine, Montesquieu, Rousseau and the Encyclopedists were placed on the shelves, along with the latest anthologies of verses and songs brought back from business trips to New Orleans. During the day, he worked hard figuring what brought a better return: indigo or sugarcane. But late at night, when the bullfrogs of the ravine had quieted and the mocking birds' trill reminded him of the European poets' beloved nightingales, the exile would reread some of Hugo's favorite lines:

> *"In a great feast one day at the Pantheon*
> *... I saw Napoleon"*

Ten months later their son was born in the same plain cabin.

Thus, here and there, Frenchmen were the keepers of a faith so contagious that in Pointe Coupee Parish a domain was named Austerlitz, and the prince of the planters, Valcour Aime, in his park known as the Versailles of Louisiana, built a rocky island that he called St. Helena. In western parishes the veterans were not so isolated. They had joined the militia and reports exchanged by different corps kept them in touch with comrades. Many were members of Masonic Lodges, not because of anti-clerical feelings, but because it served as a link between them.

They also kept contact through itinerant merchants, successors to the *coureur des bois*. Among them was one favorite. He was Jules Alexis Fecel, whose name, pronounced *Feecel* by strangers, had given rise to the often repeated joke: "Old Ficelle (string), you tie us together!"

Pale and blond, Fecel was quite different from the other Bordeaux emigrants. He had been captured in Spain and, spitting blood after his forced sojourn on British pontoons, he now had only one desire: to settle in a sunny climate. Even the Louisiana sun was not powerful enough to heal his lungs. A sedentary occupation would have hastened his death. Courageously, he bought a cart

The St. Helena Medal, presented in 1857 by Napoleon III to soldiers who had fought under Napoleon I between 1792 and 1815. The medal shown here belonged to Joseph Cherbonnier and is now in the possession of his descendant, Ben Cherbonnier of Baton Rouge, Louisiana.

(Photograph by Edgar Shore)

General Jean Joseph Humbert, intrepid but erratic personality among the exiles, eventually cast his lot with a pirate band in the Gulf of Mexico. His turbulent life ended miserably in New Orleans.

(Courtesy *Bibliothèque Nationale*, Paris, France)

Enigmatic General Charles Lallemand, leader of a group of Napoleonic exiles in the South, saw his motives challenged and eventually became the object of a violent controversy in New Orleans.

(Courtesy *Bibliothèque Nationale*, Paris, France)

*Epitaph to an Exile.
This tombstone in the cemetery
of the Church of the Assumption
in Plattenville, Louisiana,
launched the author's quest for
Napoleonic exiles in America.
Translated from the French,
the inscription reads:*

PIERRE CHARLET
BORN IN GRENOBLE, FRANCE
SOLDIER OF NAPOLEON I
DIED JAN. 3, 1866
83 YEARS OLD

*An aristocrat from Southern France and an officer in Bonaparte's
early campaigns, Garrigues de Flaugeac lived out his years in
Louisiana where he became "a virtuous and enlightened legislator
and died regretted by all good citizens," according to the
inscription on his tomb in St. Landry Cemetery in Opelousas.*

(Courtesy Opelousas *Daily World*)

The so-called Napoleon House, at the corner of *Chartres* and St. Louis streets, bears the name of the Emperor as the result of a rumor, once given wide acceptance, that Napoleon would be spirited from exile on St. Helena and brought here, the home of New Orleans Mayor Nicholas Girod.

(Courtesy Rudolf Hertzberg Collection, Special Collections Division, Tulane University Library)

This view of the area at the foot of Canal Street, drawn by George Washington Sully in 1836, shows the New Orleans Custom House (two-story structure at center) designed by Pierre Benjamin Buisson.

(Courtesy Special Collections Division, Tulane University Library)

This water color of an Indian camp on the bank of the Mississippi River was painted by Fleury Generelly as he passed the scene aboard ship.

(Courtesy Special Collections Division, Tulane University Library; a gift of Simone Delery)

and horse and kept traveling. It was not always safe and pleasant. As night fell he sometimes had to stop on the edge of a swamp. Through the grey moss hanging from branches he could see crocodiles' pointed heads. He had to stay awake to keep a fire burning to ward off wild beasts which might come and mosquitoes which always came. At other times, luck would permit him to reach the inn kept by his former companion in arms, Marcellin Garand.

"It is I, Fecel. Don't you recognize me, Lieutenant?" Fecel would ask.

"I recognize your voice," would come the reply.

Garand, from Conflans, had taken part in every campaign from 1804 to 1815. The Russian snows had made him half blind. Yet, as did the *grognards*, he grumbled but kept going. Dismissed from the army after Waterloo, he came to America. Still suffering from wounds received in Germany in 1806 and in Poland in 1812 and his eyesight being poor, he found that the only way he could make a living was to offer lodging to the few travelers passing by. He refused to ask help from his father-in-law, the proud and harsh Chevalier de Vidrine who had fled France after a tragic quarrel. Disapproving of his sister's fiancé, he killed him and forced her and the rest of the family to flee to America.

The unfortunate Josephine often said that her name, which had belonged to a repudiated Empress, was a bad omen. Secluded in her bedroom, her long tresses falling to her knees, she offered an image of despair to her bewildered young nieces. One of them had reached the ripe age of eighteen when Napoleon's defeat brought the Carabineer officer to St. Landry. The aristocratic de Vidrine forgot his prejudices. A brave lieutenant, even though he had served the usurper and opened an inn, could be an acceptable son-in-law on a new continent.

Besides, news had reached Louisiana that Colonel Raoul was now an innkeeper in Alabama and that his wife, born a marchioness, had become famous for her pancakes. Mademoiselle de Vidrine would be as good a helpmate as the marquise, with or without pancakes, yet still retain her standing.

"Where are you going from here, Fecel?" Garand asked his friend.

"First, I will go to St. Tammany Parish to see Lieutenant Samuel Stephens."

"An Englishman?"

"No, an Irish volunteer in the *Grande Armée*. He had very much the same career we had. He was wounded twice like you, was a prisoner like myself, and was put out of his regiment at the very time I was, September 1815. He came here and married a widow from Natchez, Anne McKittrick. Afterward I will go North. They are lonely up there. Some don't even get a newspaper."

"You ought to do something for them, Fecel."

Passing through New Orleans, the merchant went to call on "the Captain." For all the veterans, "the Captain" meant Benjamin Buisson.

"Could you do something for our comrades way up North? (North referred to the upper part of the state.) I went up the Red River and saw Jean David from Bordeaux. He does not look too happy."

Fecel remembered an incident, the memory of which remained with him. After nightfall had brought them from the pine grove and its cicadas to the dimly lit David cabin, the host had waited until his wife left to put little Sarah to bed. Then he motioned Fecel to follow him to the back of the room where a large canvas was hanging. Through the smoke of a resin torch one could barely perceive a greenish landscape. "What do you see?" "Trees."

Call from the Good Earth

"Look a little longer." Then Fecel saw it. On the right side of the picture was a big star above a tomb on a rocky shore. On the left, ghost-like in the foliage but becoming more distinct as one gazed at it, the silhouette of a man appeared: "*Him*, looking at his star and at his tomb." The uncanny vision was the work of a *demi-solde* and had been brought to American rolled up in some other belongings. David wished that through his daughter's care it would be passed on to other generations. His wish was granted.

With his good common sense, Fecel wondered whether it was not dangerous for anyone to remain wrapped up in a past evoked daily by the cicadas' song and a faded picture. Buisson shared his concern.

The *Frelon* (Wasp), guided by Captain Ferrand's expert hand, slowly sailed up the Mississippi, fighting the muddy surge. The ship turned into the Red River, advancing quicker on the calmer water tinted a bloody color by Texas sand. Several days after leaving New Orleans the *Frelon* had reached the Grand Ecore landing, a short distance from the former Natchitoches (Nakitosh) Post. A robust man in his early thirties was among Captain Ferrand's passengers on that autumn day of 1824. It was Benjamin Buisson, who would not have been a typical 19th century French political exile had he not tried his luck in the newspaper field. Entrusting his little family to the care of Frederic and Elizabeth, he left to reconnoiter.

On the way he heard that already a few small parishes had bilingual gazettes. Often a gazette was published by a school master who in several instances happened to be an ex-soldier. It was necessary to push farther north. The *Frelon* and the *Neptune* plied to and fro every other week. News could be exchanged, news picked up on the Natchez Trace leading to mysterious and attractive Mexico. Buisson started the bilingual *Le Courrier de Nachitoches* and, to give himself more authority, affixed to his name the title: "Publisher of the Laws of the United States."

As there were seldom laws to be printed, a great deal of space was left to acquaint readers with what was going on in Louisiana, such as the grandiose reception tendered to Lafayette in New Orleans and the endless discussions about the choice of a new state capital. On this subject, Buisson, with tongue in cheek, described each little community which boasted of being the dullest place in the South, if not in all America. Parliamentarians would be able to avoid there the temptations of New Orleans. Because of such temptations, only discreetly suggested, the big city was in danger of losing its designation as capital.

Showing insight and courage, the editor of *Le Courrier de Nachitoches* reported an incident that New Orleans newspapers had chosen to ignore. Under the signature *Ami de l'Ordre* (Friend of Order) Buisson disclosed that one night more than 300 slaves had invaded the Orleans College and had held within its gates a bacchanal that lasted until guards came to arrest 80 of them and chase the others away. In his column Buisson begged the head of the institution to offer more protection to the children entrusted to him. Buisson did not add any comment, but perhaps he thought that Orleanians may have had cause to regret Lakanal's departure.

There was in Natchitoches an Academy, a sort of High School for boys and girls (separately, of course). According to its catalog's promises, classes would be held in two languages. Buisson discovered that there was no French professor and stirred public opinion. He wrote:

"The head of a family who neglects to teach French to his children is not only a bad citizen, he is also a bad father." To uphold his opinions he presented not only sentimental reasons, but practical ones as well. Being practical himself, he decided that the best gift he could offer the Natchitoches residents would be a French teacher. If only he could locate Victor Cherbonnier whose double ambition had been to rule over a household and a classroom! He found Cherbonnier who, with the Creole wife of his dreams, was delighted to accept the teaching assignment.

From that point on the Academy had a French professor who sometimes interrupted the explanation of a grammatical rule with a lively anecdote: "When we camped near Dresden..."

Often at night Cherbonnier exchanged reminiscences with the lawyer Laurent, who had settled there after his flight from Champ d'Asile. He was so lonely, but he was largely to blame. He forbade his wife to wear white as being too conspicuous. One evening he saw her coming down the tall staircase, her long brown curls caressing the décolleté of a snow white dress. Enraged, he slapped her delicate face. No words passed between them but later, returning from a business trip, he found an empty house. Natchitoches, buzzing with gossips, later learned that Mrs. Laurent was making a living for herself and her three young children, thanks to the Pension de Jeunes Demoiselles she had opened in New Orleans.

Often on Thursdays, when the school was closed, according to French custom, Cherbonnier left on horseback to visit his colleague Adolphe Lafargue from the Pyrenees. Son of one of Napoleon's colonels, Adolphe hardly had a taste of battlefields when the Imperial regime came to an end and was barely over eighteen when he came to America. He launched into a teaching career in which he was going to make a name for himself and for his descendants. He also cooperated heartily with a young missionary who, upon his arrival from France, found fifty marriages to bless in one day and countless children to baptize in the improvised wooden chapel among the pine woods. Perhaps Father Martin's fighting spirit was akin to Lafargue's and when the energetic priest became Bishop of Natchitoches, the French teacher often rode along the trail, passing through forests and swamps to confer with him about the building of a church in the newly-born community of Marksville. To Marksville Lafargue had given its first semi-public, semi-private high school. Unless a child was recognized as an indigent he had to pay a small tuition fee; often children from the surrounding countryside boarded with the school master's family.

Church and school were not enough to satisfy Lafargue's ambition. He decided that the inhabitants of Avoyelles Parish deserved to have a newspaper and he founded a bilingual one. He called it *Le Villageois* for the French readers and *The Villager* for the English-speaking part of the population. It was very much like the newspaper that Benjamin Buisson had launched in Natchitoches. After he felt sure a successor would continue his task, however, Buisson left. The picturesque little town reflecting its shops in the reddish water of the Cane River could not retain the Parisian. He was longing for a bigger city and for his home enriched by the presence of newly born Sophie.

IX

Printing and Planning

"*Dans la plus affreuse misère*
(In the most frightful misery)

"*De vieux soldats passent leurs jours*
(Old soldiers spend their days)

"*Eux qui faisaient trembler naguère*
(Trembled under their power)

"*Les rois, les peuples et les cours*
(Once, kings, peoples and courts)

"*Hélas, les fiers enfants d'Arcole*
(Alas, poor Arcole's children)

"*Qui souvent n'ont rien à manger*
(Often have nothing to eat)

"*Savez-vous ce qui les console?*
(Do you know what comforts them?)

"*Une chanson de Béranger.*"
(A song by Béranger.)

Loud voices repeated the refrain: "A song by Béranger!" "Well done, Montmain! Boismare, when are you going to print this in your *Passe Tems*?"

Such a scene could have taken place any day of the late 1820s in a shop located a few yards from St. Louis

Cathedral. At 137 Chartres Street a Parisian bibliophile, Antoine Louis Boismare, piled up sketches, bottles of India ink, rolls of wallpapers with exotic designs and books on rarely dusted shelves. The advantages of this *cabinet de lecture* and its varied contents were offered not merely to Orleanians. Numerous advertisements in city and parish newspapers let planters and farmers know that for a yearly payment of $18 they would receive a carefully padlocked case containing fifteen volumes which, as soon as they were read, could be exchanged for fifteen others. Boismare and his staff, through their choice of material, spread their opinions and their tastes. The nature of these opinions was clearly indicated in the review Boismare published on the 1st, 10th, 15th and 20th of each month. The *Passe Tems* was subtitled: "*Macédoine Politique et Littéraire.*"

What emanated from this so-called mixture was a strong Bonapartist flavor. It appeared as if the editors, scissors in hand, had clipped from the international press any article referring to Imperial France. There was no dearth of such contributions in the years 1827–29 when the *Passe Tems* flourished. Readers were told that in Paris there came out in succession a history of the Spanish War by General Foy and a history of the Russian campaign by the Marquis de Chambray, whose work was compared with de Segur's. There were also *1812* by Baron Fain, the Emperor's former secretary and archivist, and *Anecdotes* by de Beausset, prefect of the palace, who began with the remark: "No one is a hero to his valet with the exception of Napoleon."

Dr. Antommarchi's description of the St. Helena prisoner's last days must have moved the Orleanians. If they preferred a lighter vein, they could read fragments of *18 Brumaire*, a play staged in the poor lodging of a thin, fiery lieutenant named Bonaparte. As should have been expected, Napoleon's writings, from a naive little fable composed at Brienne to the *Mémorial,* were given a prominent place. Indeed, the *Mémorial* was the most advertised book, not only in Boismare's review but in all New Orleans papers. It found its way to every corner of Louisiana where, more than a century later, it still could be seen in the rich Marquis de Tiernant's library, on Wartelle's shelves in the home still standing near Bayou Cocodrie, or in the large armoire where Pierre Charlet stored his treasures at Plattenville.

Often a Paris publication was a source of commentaries. The story of Colonel Duval who boasted of being Napoleon's illegitimate son aroused sympathy for "young Leon." A critic compared the Emperor to a vast sea covered with thousands of vessels of all nationalities, the vessels being the historians and novelists His Majesty had inspired. "Only a Scotchman was shipwrecked on this Ocean of Glory," it was written. This was a reference to Sir Walter Scott. In him, "the English baronet had killed the historian, he had prostituted his pen."

Poems written on both sides of the Atlantic often were offered to the *Passe Tems* subscribers. Famous names were thrown pell mell with others so obscure it was difficult to find out whether they were "French from France" or not. Who, for example, was Adolphe Nicolas, author of the *Chants du Siècle* (Songs of the Century)? In a dramatic epilogue he portrayed Napoleon entering eternity at the head of his legions. By daring to suggest they might have to wait a thousand years before the Gates of Heaven would open to them, he displeased many readers.

"Look at what I have received from Philadelphia!" enthusiastic Fleury Generelly exclaimed one day on entering Boismare's shop. He displayed *Ode aux Défenseurs de la Nouvelle Orléans* (Ode to the Defenders of New Orleans), dedicated to him by his friend Simon Chaudron. The latter had been one of the first victims of the San Domingo debacle to reach the American continent. He experienced a day of fame when at the Amenity Lodge of Philadelphia he read "Brother Washington's Funeral Eulogy." Later on, Chaudron launched *L'Abeille Américaine* (The American Bee), the industrious insect having probably been selected as the name because it had been one of the Imperial emblems. After Waterloo, still living in the North, he invited his fellow countrymen to form a colony:

> *And Kings in your turn,*
> *In your rustic estates*
> *Only laws and gods*
> *Will be your masters.*

Setting an example, he acquired some shares in the Wine and Olive enterprise in Alabama. In 1818, *L'Abeille Américaine* having ceased buzzing, Chaudron settled in Marengo County, Alabama. From there and from nearby Mobile, while he progressively lost his eyesight, he established contact with New Orleans comrades. It was probably under his directive that in 1827 another San Domingo refugee founded *L'Abeille de la Nouvelle Orléans*, which, as a phenomenon in the annals of the local press, would survive for almost a century in spite of the stings of a later day rival: *Le Frelon* (The Wasp).

Simon Chaudron, either under his own name or a transparent nom de plume, "Old Kettle," sent frequent contributions to the *Passe Tems*. Most of them were violent, sometimes humorous satires of the Bourbon regime. *La Fête de François* (François' Feast Day) added a sentimental note showing an older soldier desperately trying to reach the young Duke of Reichstadt in Schoenbrunn Palace to give him his father's sword. This forerunner of Rostand's *L'Aiglon* was deeply appreciated, and Orleanians took the almost blind poet to their hearts.

French authors were not quoted according to their literary merits but according to their political opinions. Chateaubriand, whose *De Buonaparte et des Bourbons* had not been forgiven, could not expect a good press.

Furthermore, romanticism was looked upon with misgiving. While second-rate pamphleteers were abundantly praised, Lamartine received lukewarm notices. Victor Hugo's statement: *"J'aurais été soldat, si je n'étais poète"* (I would have been a soldier if I had not been a poet) was widely memorized. Readers were reminded that the author's father had commanded a division during the difficult Spanish campaign. Thus "Hugo's name will not perish" sustained as it was by a general's stars.

Popular taste placed Beranger even higher and his glory reflected upon Guillaume Montmain. In both songwriters there were three tendencies to satisfy Orleanians' tastes: a mischievous Voltairian attitude toward religious authorities, a *joie de vivre* that neither fevers, fires, nor floods had ever extinguished and a stubborn Napoleonic faith.

An example of the latter was found in an advertisement printed in the *Passe Tems*. Messieurs Dorfeuille and Turpin, having realized that reptiles and sea shells had lost their appeal, announced that their Musée was now displaying a huge panorama of the Waterloo battlefield and St. Helena's rocky shores. As an added attraction, there would be "life-size Venuses." Who could resist finding his way to the Musée?

But in Boismare's shop one did not always live in the past, whether mythologic or Napoleonic. It was necessary to take care of the present, and the present was always cloudy for a Louisiana publisher. Reviews and gazettes were often launched by Europeans possessing great initiative, small capital and a mediocre acquaintance with the public. They disappeared as quickly as human lives during an epidemic. Toward the end of 1829 the *Passe Tems* was about to breathe its last, either for lack of funds or because a new venture was exercising its magic.

Journalistic instinct cannot be smothered. After Benjamin Buisson passed his *Courrier de Nachitoches* into other hands and went home, he was a constant visitor to 137 Chartres Street. Soon a publishing firm opened under the name of Boismare and Buisson.

The first author they published was Pierre Cherbonnier, the same Pierre Cherbonnier who for a while had been a sort of accountant at Jean Laffite's Grand Terre headquarters and later, as the *Ami des Lois* editor, had become entangled in the Lallemand controversies. Deciding to become an educator, he realized that the text books acquired from France did not answer the young Orleanians' needs. A greater number of Americans had been attracted by the port. They made a greater effort to learn French, which was necessary to gain access to many homes and offices, than the French population did to learn English. What was needed was a book elementary enough not to discourage the learner, but complete enough to serve as a Bible for any gentleman desiring to absorb more culture. Finding advanced subscribers for the publication was an easy task. Therefore Boismare and Buisson successfully published the *Alphabet*, as it was modestly titled.

It was a copious volume where practical notions of arithmetic and geography and the rules for the composition of an epigram or of an epitaph could be found. One can visualize Colonel Cuvelier, in one hand the *Alphabet*,

Printing and Planning 131

in the other the little rod used to call day-dreamers to attention, walking back and forth in the classrooms of his Collège de la Louisiane dictating: "Fifty-six yards of black velvet from Rome, on the Tiber, capital of Italy, at three dollars a yard, made $168." He would pause to extract a pinch of tobacco from his snuff box and continue: "Three barrels of good wine from Buda, located on the Danube, capital of Hungary, at 28 *piastres* a barrel, make 84 *piastres*." Through such a method, the pupils learned they could order bear skins from Columbus, Ohio, wild geese from Cahawba, the Alabama capital, or hams from Frankfort, Kentucky. As to their obtaining tafia (in later years, one would hope), they would find it on their own wharves.

At the same time, the oldest among the *jeunes demoiselles* of Madame de Perdreauville's Academy, having carefully placed their petit-point in their desks, were meandering through the intricacies of "the logic, grammatical and metaphysical analysis of Madame Deshoulierès' charming idyl called *Les Moutons* (The Sheep). Elsewhere masters explaining that the subjunctive mood expresses emotion or desire were grateful for the example given by comrade Cherbonnier: "Everyone wishes that Napoleon's body be returned to France."

However, printing the *Alphabet,* the *Manuel de Géographie Elementaire,* or the *Life of Père Antoine,* who had just died, did not fill Buisson and Boismare's pockets. Boismare sailed for France, taking with him a valuable manuscript, *Le Journal Historique de l'Etablissement des Français,* by Bernard de la Harpe. He was going to have it printed in Paris. He left his partner fighting creditors who claimed Sophie's dowry. A Spanish law cited by the adverse parties stated that the marriage contract, as it was, did not furnish definite proof that the few hundred dollars were the bride's personal property. The Buissons lost their suit but Benjamin did not lose courage. He was still adventurous enough to start a *Journal du Commerce,* which had the unusual fate of surviving four years.

Amid his financial debacle and his efforts to make another attempt in the journalistic world, Buisson still found time to appear with military bearing and full trappings at the head of his battalion. He was there when the Legionnaires, with crape armbands and crape on the pommel of their swords, drums muffled by black cloth, marched in Père Antoine's funeral. The whole city attended the service, even the Free Masons, which gave rise to an unconfirmed rumor that the Capuchin monk had been one of the brothers.

Then 1830 saw another ceremony that stirred the city's emotions. After the priest came the pirate. Banks closed and flags were lowered when the news came that Dominique You had died in his humble home. Orleanians felt remorse and gave the dead man the attention they had refused him toward the end of his life. Frenchmen remembered that it was during Bonaparte's San Domingo expedition that the buccaneer had learned to lay and aim cannons. Never had Buisson's gunners fired salvos with more ardor.

In the St. Louis cemetery, rich and poor, whites and blacks pressed forward, crushing wreaths and flowers brought there earlier on the Toussaint feast day. They were eager to hear the eulogy to be pronounced in front of the plain pine coffin placed on the pile of bricks, so red under the luminous sky. A paper clumsily held in his big trembling fingers, Simon Laignel came forward. He was going to speak in the name of all the seamen (on such an occasion any word smacking of piracy would have been in bad taste) who had traveled the Caribbean Sea in the Gulf of Mexico as the deceased's devoted companions. Everyone knew the part Captain You had played during the Chalmette Battle, Laignel declared, but were the Orleanians aware of what else he had done for them? More than once, when the Mississippi River flooded fields, uprooted homes and sent them drifting away with terrified inhabitants on their roofs, Dominique had come to the rescue. Answering his call, his former crew had rushed forward. The resulting flotilla of skiffs, canoes and pirogues had saved many lives.

The speech was long, yet more was expected. Had not the name of You formerly entered hushed talks about a St. Helena plot? If he had been the leader or one of the leaders, would not Simon Laignel mention it? Nine years after Napoleon's death this revelation would not have endangered anyone and would have added an aura to the honored dead man. Yet, nothing was said about it. Later on, the following words were carved on the tombstone:

Intrépide guerrier sur la terre et sur l'onde
(Fearless warrior on land and on sea)

Il sut dans cent combats signaler sa valeur
(In a hundred fights he displayed his courage)

Et ce nouveau Bayard sans reproche et sans peur
(And this new knight without fear and without reproach)

Aurait pu sans trembler voir s'écrouler le monde.
(Without trembling could have seen the world crumble.)

At that moment, New Orleans was carried away by such a Francophile feeling that German and Irish newcomers, perhaps out of jealousy, called it "the French craze." What had brought it on? Probably the three-day revolution which had led to the removal of Charles X from his throne. The new ruler was not unknown. Older citizens remembered the visit he and his frail younger brother had paid them at the turn of the century. De Marigny had been their host and in his usual lordly style had discreetly slipped some money to the exiled adolescents. Was it not to be expected that the city named in honor of a former Duke of Orleans should extend its allegiance to this other Duke of Orleans, now King of France under the name of Louis Philippe I?

The Bourbons' fall brought the tricolor flag back to the top of ship masts, flying openly, not ushered in at the last moment so that the Captain would not incur the Consul's wrath. Newspapers announced that the first ship entering the port with the red, white and blue would receive an official welcome. The officers and crew would be entertained by the city. From that day all eyes were turned toward the river. At last, slowly gliding above the levee which screened the hull from view, the tricolor appeared in the sky. Messengers flew to the office of Buisson, who rapidly gave orders to his men. At the same time, a signal was sent to the restaurant already selected—the best, of course. When the captain and his aides came down the gangway they were dumbfounded to see a delegation in blue and gold uniforms with fanfares blasting the *Marseillaise,* waiting to escort them to a banquet. "You should tell the Parisians how happy we are," the delighted guests heard again and again.

They certainly would tell, but it would take months and months since the merchant ship had to unload, then reload there and in many harbors before returning to Le Havre. What one ought to do is send a delegation over there, enthusiastic Orleanians thought and said. In haste, Buisson called a Legion meeting. Congratulations and

Printing and Planning 135

wishes to the new government were carefully worded. Who would take them? Quite naturally, the men turned toward their leader. Gravely, he declined the honor. The passing of years had emptied the Cloître St. Méry residence and filled the St. Philippe home with mouths to feed. Yet, he must have felt sad when he bade goodbye to the ex-artillery lieutenant and former Collège d'Orléans professor sailing on the *Attakapas* with comrade St. Maurice. Holding the banner of the Louisiana Legion, Pierre Guillot would be received at the Tuileries and, with St. Maurice, present New Orleans' homage to Louis Philippe I.

Their mission accomplished, the two messengers returned praising the new regime's liberal views. It was an invitation for some of the exiles whose homesickness was still latent to return to France. So the number of the ex-soldiers dwindled, but the remaining ones closed ranks and kept alive their former loyalties.

The news of the Duke of Reichstadt's death in 1832 did not bring the shock that might have been expected. The *Courrier de la Louisiane* reproduced a pathetic article from the Paris *Temps* retracing the unfortunate child's story from the day his mother took him to Vienna. Metternich and the Austrian court atmosphere smothered him. News of the Bourbons' fall woke him up. "Suddenly, July 1830, his depression was followed by exaltation, a fever brought about by a continuous delirious imagination was going to kill him. He thought only of military drills. His young and frail voice broke down in repeated orders called out in an 18 degree cold."

The article compared Napoleon's son to other political victims. "New Iron Mask, he was walled in." Then, came the description of months of illness during which care was denied him. "And you, poor child of glory, you died abandoned!" According to a letter sent from Austria, a French artist who had been able to reach the prince was given this message: "Tell the Column (Vendome) that the regret not to be able to embrace it is what is killing me."

A selection from a Northern paper was less sympathetic. According to the article, the former *Roi de Rome* had not inherited his father's great qualities; he was merely an "amiable young man" who resembled Marie Louise. To have such an heir was Napoleon's punishment. For what sin? The *Courrier de la Louisiane* enlightened its readers on the point. The unforgivable fault was his repudiation of Josephine.

Perhaps because the Duke of Reichstadt had not been the Creole's son, he was not mourned for long. Another event had interfered. The news had arrived during the cruelest summer ever experienced. "Bring your dead . . . your dead," chanted tumbrel drivers carting corpses away. When yellow fever killed four or five children in a family, the death of an unknown prince in far-away Schoenbrunn had little meaning for grieving parents.

New Orleans' population had greatly increased since the first *demi-soldes* had landed at the end of 1815. Sugar and cotton enriched planters who brought money to banks and spent freely in the big port. The city spread fanshaped, and the French Quarter was only a little square at the end of what would be the handle. Already, to the east, streets were cut through Bernard de Marigny's property. No doubt, the *bon vivant* suggested the street names: Amour, Musique, Poésie, Mystère and Venus. Good Children Street probably was chosen to balance Craps, named after the dice game introduced by Marigny

Printing and Planning

and equally loved by whites and blacks. There was also the long Champ Elysées which brought joy to French hearts, although the resemblance did not extend beyond the name.

In that section called Chantilly, and later Gentilly, however, princely de Marigny was not the only one to own land. There was his counterpart, Antoine Michoud—as obscure as Marigny was flamboyant—a French soldier from Lyons who came after Waterloo, and opened a bric-a-brac and art store on Royal Street near St. Louis. Unmarried, unsociable and eccentric, he saved his money *sou par sou* (cent by cent) and acquired a vast wasteland between Lake Borgne and Lake Pontchartrain which many years later would bring a fortune to his Lyons heirs. Land rich, he died a pauper in 1862. It took three quarters of a century and a missile complex to make his name world famous.

The business section was overflowing Canal Street, reaching upriver. Faubourg St. Mary was no longer large enough to accommodate all the residences needed. Some were built a distance from the river, each one screened by trees and creating a diversity of architecture that would become known as the Garden District. Soon this region would cease to be the residence of only the English, German and Irish people. A few Creole families, attracted by wider streets and space where magnolias and evergreen oaks could be planted, were beginning to leave the Vieux Carré. The remaining families did not hide their indignation: "Cousin Odile is building a house uptown. What do you think of that, *chère*? What kind of husbands will she find for her daughters among those strangers?"

Higher still, in the convexity of the crescent embraced by the Mississippi, wild nature was attacked. There were lots which Creoles had bought at low prices out of the Jesuits' domain when their Order had to leave Louisiana. Such land, only three or four miles from the city proper, was too valuable to be made into pastures or fields. It was in those sections called Jefferson and Lafayette that Benjamin Buisson was called to work as surveyor and engineer, following in the footsteps of other Frenchmen such as Pauger who had left their mark on the city map.

The new Director of Public Works began to encounter difficulties. Problems sprang up, less from the rarity of building material or the harshness of the summers than from human interference. Sloping down from the top of the embankment to the water's edge was an often inundated strip of land called the *batture*. The state, which owned the waterways, attempted to put its grip on the *batture*. Poor people had squatted there for years and felt they were the sole proprietors. Buisson was chosen as an umpire. Sometimes the dissatisfied party would not accept his verdict. Lawyers had to be consulted. Thus the signature of Benjamin Buisson appeared on a number of lawsuits. In addition, he had to fight for his own interests. For him and his brother Frederic, who had become notary public and sheriff, Louisiana was decidedly their permanent home. For themselves and their numerous children, each one of them forming a new tie with their adopted country, they bought a piece of land when the price was reasonable.

Benjamin had left St. Philip Street and had built a larger residence in Faubourg Plaisance near the section on which he would leave his imprint. Often he worked late at night on the plan of that swampy part which would have to be drained. A wide avenue would be opened from the Mississippi River to what was vaguely referred to as "the woods," a sort of maquis stretching toward Lake

Printing and Planning 139

Pontchartrain. Lateral streets, then, would have to be cut.

Lines on a sheet of paper representing the arteries and veins of a large city take life only when they cease to be nameless. "What are you going to call your streets?" a colleague, Joseph Pilié, asked Benjamin.

Buisson bent over his plans with fervor. The realistic and sentimental elements in him had to find satisfaction. At last he displayed his map. When Frederic saw it, he must have recalled the time when the two little boys listened to soldiers' stories on their way back from school.

The wide avenue was called Napoleon. For the adjacent streets the ex-officer of the Imperial Army had chosen Marengo, Milan, Jena and Austerlitz. There was also Berlin, to celebrate its capture by the French, and Valence, because from that garrison young Bonaparte had started his ascent toward glory. They were names for a virgin region that shovels and pick-axes soon would attack. Homes would be built and people would repeat those words . . . Napoleon, Marengo, Milan . . . and perhaps unknowingly pay tribute to the past. The former *demi-solde* successfully had blended his work and his dream. Others had celebrated Napoleon in their poems and songs. Benjamin Buisson had carved the legend into Louisiana soil.

X

Dr. Antommarchi and Prince Murat

WHILE BUISSON PLANNED A COMMUNITY, another Napoleonic soldier entered Louisiana. Claudius Crozet also had graduated from the Ecole Polytechnique, but when Benjamin Buisson studied there, Crozet already was an artillery captain attached to the Imperial Guard. Taken prisoner during the Russian campaign, he met a compassionate family who obtained permission to employ him. During his leisure hours he wrote a Russian grammar. When he returned to France, he was awarded the Lily decoration by Louis XVIII, but nothing could induce him to serve the Bourbons. He left Europe on the ship with General Simon Bernard, who gave him advice and letters of recommendation.

Because of his mentor's influence, he was invited to join a group of carefully selected professors forming the faculty of the military academy being organized at West Point. One day, he faced a class of adolescents bewildered by his broken English. No textbook was available to breach the language gap. Rapidly Crozet walked to a seldom-used blackboard. "Attention!" he ordered. Chalk in hand, he traced geometrical figures and with few words and many gestures solved intricate problems.

His courage and his skill were widely admired. A

Dr. Antommarchi and Prince Murat 141

report written by his supervisor in 1822 mentioned that "Captain Crozet is by far the best mathematician in the United States." Among his pupils was young Henry Latrobe, son of the architect residing at the Tremoulet Hotel. Later on, having become an architect himself, the former West Point cadet wrote about this French professor who, unexpectedly, would interrupt an explanation to reminisce about one of his campaigns: "The anecdotes by which he illustrated his teaching were a great deal more interesting than the science of wars and fortifications."

With mathematical precision, the learned and vivacious instructor divided his life into an engineering and professorial career. He devoted the same number of years he had spent at West Point to construction works in Virginia. It was at this time that he received an invitation to head Jefferson College in Louisiana. Lakanal had been *persona non grata*, but it did not naturally follow that other educators from the same country would prove as tactless. Furthermore, among the Board members, mostly Creoles, who desired to see a new institution surpass the defunct Collège d'Orléans was Dominique Burthe, and he put in a good word for a former Army comrade.

Jefferson College was located a few miles above New Orleans facing the protective levee. Claudius Crozet went to live in the long building with tall white columns, less a school in appearance than a rich planter's mansion. No walls encircled the large grounds shaded by oak trees and gigantic magnolias. "What a contrast with our prison-like lycées!" Crozet must have thought.

A few years later a Breton priest, Abbé de la Fouchardière, who under the pen name of René de Sennegy wrote a history of St. Michel Parish, drew a parallel between Jefferson College and the Dijon Lycée in Burgundy, described by the well-known Catholic orator, Lacordaire. "At Jefferson and at Dijon, there were superior minds." Here, de Sennegy mentioned Crozet. "But a Master, a very great Master was lacking: God." The gentle Abbé insisted on the harsh discipline of the Louisiana school, offering a sinister picture of professors moving about, revolvers in hand. He neglected to say against whom such a weapon was used or whether it was used at all. It is probable that the French officer's influence was instrumental in ushering in the military discipline Bonaparte had imposed on his lycées. However, the Jefferson students' fathers did not object to it. They knew that at home their sons had been spoiled. How could it be otherwise with the Negroes' servility, always eager to please the "little master," and the Creole mothers' adulation?

In any case, Colonel Crozet's value was fully appreciated. When he left he did so of his own volition and regrets were expressed by all who had come in contact with him. But three years in such an isolated spot were enough for such a restless man. For his sole diversion he walked daily on the top of the levee, noticing here a part of the bank eaten up by the grey waves, there the tiny beach where floatsam had piled up. These sights made him think of another task toward which he would like to turn his quenchless energy.

There were two Polytechnicians in New Orleans who would follow in Simon Bernard's steps and continue the effort to make communication safer and swifter. It was a ceaseless struggle to keep sediment from choking the mouths of the Mississippi River and to preserve at least one passage deep enough to permit large ships to reach the harbor. Would it not be less costly to dig a canal that would help generations to come? Benjamin Buisson, now Chief Engineer of the State of Louisiana,

Dr. Antommarchi and Prince Murat 143

submitted a project. But it only added its weight to the piles of documents turning yellow in the Federal archives.

During this period Claudius Crozet was making a study of smaller streams. If they could be free from obstruction, shipments of cotton, sugarcane, and indigo would reach the city much faster. The transportation of products to general stores, the villages' commercial axis, also would be enhanced. Colonel Crozet, as he was now known, wrote many reports asking for funds, which he sometimes obtained. As a result, the Atchafalaya, the Homochitto and other streams with Indian names were opened to regular navigation. The former Bonapartist officer disciplined even waterways!

Boldly, he thought of another enterprise. Why not enable Louisiana to profit from the newly invented railroad? Orleanians raised their eyebrows. Instead of spending so much money on those *chemins à coulisses,* why not build a roof on top of the main roads to maintain them "pleasantly dry," they suggested. The Colonel remained adamant. Louisianians should see what railroads had to offer. A report to the Head Engineer of the State made public by the *Bee,* on January 11, 1834 and signed C. Crozet announced to the Orleanians that twenty miles of tracks were being laid between Port Hudson on the Mississippi River and the little inland community of Clinton, 70 miles northwest of New Orleans. It was but an example, just enough to calm fears.

Again, the engineer was at work, not in an office, but out among the laborers, calling orders in French, English and Negro dialect, gesticulating as vigorously as when he commanded his gunners on a battlefield. Pick-axes were striking the heavy mud following the rhythm of the blacks' song. The chief yelled and scolded but did not handle a whip. *"Mossieu Cozet, li pas mauvais!"* (Mr.

Crozet, not bad!) Faces shiny with sweat would smile at him. "What is this man up to now?" passersby wondered. The answer would fill them with joy.

As soon as the hot weather set in, Lake Pontchartrain became the big attraction. In less than fifteen minutes, one was now able to cover the four and a half miles which separated them from salty breezes. The tall chimney of "Smoky Mary," the narrow locomotive, showered the travelers with soot, but on arriving at Milneburg they would rush for a dip, modesty being protected by the four walls of tiny cabins built on piles. When visitors came from other states, they were told proudly that New Orleans possessed the second railroad ever built in the United States, thanks to an officer of Napoleon's army.

At the height of the esteem he had inspired, Colonel Crozet moved away but still kept land and friends in Louisiana. Very likely, his recommendation brought South one of his colleagues, since Albert Jumel had belonged to the same army and had taught at West Point. During his youth, Jumel spent hours under the guidance of the greatest swordman of France, La Boissière. The skill he had gained gave the exiled *demi-solde* an opportunity for a livelihood. For a while he was employed in Charles Lallemand's school in New York. Then, bolstered by flattering references, he became swordmaster at West Point. After a few years there, he came South. Although still young when he died, he left a family. His home became one of those islets of French influence not far from Jefferson College where he had taught and where his friend Claudius Crozet had acted as president.

"In France, everything ends with songs," a State Minister had said during the *Ancien Régime*. It could have been as true in 19th century Louisiana.

Dr. Antommarchi and Prince Murat

"*Allons, Français, Américains*
(Come on, French, Americans,)
"*Hâtons-nous, courons au rivage*
(Let us hasten to the shore)
"*Pour exalter de nos refrains*
(To celebrate by our songs)
"*L'homme d'honneur et de courage.*
(The man of courage and honor.)

The *Courrier's* readers were invited to sing this stanza to welcome Dr. Antommarchi. His name was quite familiar; it had been mentioned often and always with sympathy during the Emperor's imprisonment. The Corsican surgeon's difficulties with his English colleague, Francis Burton, and with Sir Hudson Lowe had been deplored. His frantic efforts to obtain sulphate of lime and chemicals in order to mix a substance plastic enough to take an imprint of the dead Napoleon's features had been praised. After he went back to France it took him twelve years to get the mask cast in bronze. He finally succeeded, it was said, with Louis Philippe's help. Yet, his help had not been enough in other matters. On September 2, 1834 he wrote Marshal Bertrand, also a witness to the Emperor's last moments, explaining why he was leaving France:

> "The Emperor Napoleon had in his last will assured my future and success. Obstacles which he could not foresee prevented the fulfillment of his kind intentions toward me. The steps which I had taken in order to secure their execution have been scoffed at. My rights and titles have been ignored and I now find myself compelled to resort to law. It would be too painful to me to witness those legal proceedings. I, therefore, with deep regret, leave

France, and I hope, *Monsieur le Maréchal,* that you will not disapprove of the motives that have made me take this resolution."

It was learned in the United States that on September 21 the *Salem,* sailing from Le Havre, had Dr. Francesco Antommarchi on board. About six weeks later, men on the lookout rode at break-neck speed to New Orleans shouting that the *Salem* was coming up the river.

At the Place d'Armes, Benjamin Buisson's cannoneers were awaiting a signal, singing a song to "the greatest of heros." When the Captain gave the order, the refrain was heard once again: "Who gathers the best laurels?" A hundred-and-one gun salute announced the landing of the former physician of His Imperial Majesty.

Francesco Antommarchi appeared, a man of medium build with a round face framed by whiskers. His sad eyes and expression of bitterness lighted up when he saw the welcoming committee. With great pomp he was escorted to the Théâtre d'Orléans where his colleague, Felix Formento, gave an oration. That night French veterans requested the honor of calling on him. Gravely they asked questions about their beloved *"Petit Caporal's"* last hours. With his strong Corsican accent, Antommarchi related anecdotes. "They listened with the deepest religious silence and showing the most sincere emotion," the *Abeille de la Nouvelle Orléans* reported the following day. From time to time, the narrator had to pause. Through the window opened on the soft November night William Tell's Overture and the cymbals of *Le Dieu et la Bayadère* (The God and the Bayadere) frequently drowned his voice. The Orleans Theater's artists were serenading him. From time to time men assembled on the *banquette* singing *la Marseillaise* at the top of their voices.

Dr. Antommarchi and Prince Murat

Antommarchi listened, smiling at the words, "the day of glory has come!"

During the *Salem's* voyage the *Abeille* had printed Antommarchi's parting letter to Bertrand, so Orleanians knew why he had left France. They were proud to see that of all the cities in the United States he had chosen New Orleans. Was it partially because of its reputation for hospitality? The citizens outdid themselves. Antommarchi, overcome by such respect and friendship, decided to offer the precious death mask to the city. The distinguished Creole mayor, Denis Prieur, accepted the gift in a letter the newspapers reproduced: "Virtue, genius, glory have always excited admiration on our republican soil, moreover, the grandiose image of Napoleon deserves our gratitude. To him, the shores of the Mississippi owe their liberty. It is thanks to him that under the Stars and Stripes' protection, they have enjoyed the benefits of freedome and democracy." So, in pompous language, Bonaparte was being thanked for having abandoned Louisiana!

On a Sunday the bronze mask was solemnly presented to the city. The Legionnaires assembled at the Place d'Armes and marched to the donor's residence. Eight of them raised on their shoulders the shield on which the mask had been placed. Then the procession, headed by Governor Andre Bienvenu Roman, the Mayor, Federal officers, and representatives of the clergy and the judiciary slowly walked to the Cabildo. There, in the Sala Capitular where the Louisiana transfer had been signed, new thanks to the Corsican doctor and new tributes to the Emperor were expressed. In the name of the city one of the dignitaries gave voice to the wish that Dr. Francisco Antommarchi would choose New Orleans as his permanent residence.

It was no wonder that after such a long ceremony, the public rushed to a spectacle highly recommended by their local newspapers: "An animated panorama of different scenes of the great Napoleon's life, with accompaniment by a military band."

More surprising than any morsel thrown to readers eager to hear about the Imperial era was a short article published December 8 in the *Abeille* for which the editor declined any responsibility: "Napoleon Frederick Buonaparte, son of His Majesty Napoleon I, has warned the public through the Baltimore's *Daily Advertiser* . . . that the motives which made him adopt the name of Jean Baptiste Tournaire having ceased, he has taken again his family name and as soon as it will be possible for him to return to France he will let the public know the reasons which justify his conduct." Nothing else about the identity and actions of this Napoleon Frederick Buonaparte appeared in the Louisiana press. About the same time, a few lines stated that the Emperor himself had been seen in Alexandria, a town in the central part of the state. In these cases, readers were keen enough to guess that adventurers were trying to take advantage of the Napoleonic enthusiasm that Antommarchi's visit had brought to a new height.

Unfortunately the Corsican surgeon did not understand that it would be better for him not to wear out his welcome. An Orleanian crowd, sensitive as any Latin crowd, was quick to applaud, but quicker still to detect any flaw. Antommarchi would not long be able to hide his limitations behind the bronze mask. Nineteenth century physicians did not hesitate to attract clientele by advertising the marvelous treatments they had to offer. A Dr. Lalaurie, for example, boasted that in practically no time he could straighten a hunchback. But the newcomer

Dr. Antommarchi and Prince Murat 149

went a step farther. He announced that he was opening two offices, one for the patients able to pay, another one for the poor. The latter cleverly was located in former Mayor Nicholas Girod's home, surrounded by Bonapartist mementoes. With such a background how could anyone forget that a doctor who had attended Napoleon deigned to take care of the underprivileged?

Physicians whispered that this way of profiting through his past was not ethical, that advertising one's good deeds was not true charity, that the ceaseless publicity about the *Mémoires* he had written and the St. Helena pictures displayed in the "paying office" were too mercenary. Arguments pro and con were flying in Felix Formento's pharmacy. And Dr. Formento could show his diplomas. Was there any proof that Antommarchi had even studied anatomy? For years he had dissected corpses, but what experience had he with the living? Why had Madame Mère chosen him as her son's physician? Perhaps old Laetitia had been attracted by the Corsican accent that would remind the prisoner of his native Ajaccio. Perhaps for the same reason she had selected for him an elderly Italian chaplain whose presence at Longwood was almost unbearable to Napoleon. Furthermore, had not Antommarchi himself been received rather coolly by the patient, who rebelled against the treatment given to him? Had he ever been mentioned in the Emperor's will as he stated?

The confidence spontaneously granted the voyager when he stepped off the *Salem* was melting away. The epithet, "quack," probably pronounced for the first time by a jealous colleague, was repeated throughout the city. The ending would be the same as for Eudes de Gentilly and Lakanal, Orleanians predicted. They were right. For three years Antommarchi fought back criticisms and slanders. With shoulders bent and eyes averted, he looked for friends and found none. Even his St. Helena anecdotes failed to attract listeners. Yet, the same people in the evening would flock to the Théâtre d'Orléans to admire the *Illusions de la Fantasmagorie* which projected on a white sheet the gigantic shadow of a symbolic France weeping over Napoleon's tomb.

One day someone noticed that the long wooden shutters of the doctor's two offices were tightly closed. He had left for Mexico. A few years afterward a brief note in the *Gazette* mentioned that Francesco Antommarchi had drowned in the course of his travels.

There was never an Antommarchi Street in New Orleans, but another visitor belonging to the same Napoleonic era was responsible for a name that Buisson or one of his assistants wrote down on a map. This newcomer, with broad forehead, piercing grey eyes and thin lips, must have attracted curious glances. Veterans passing him must have experienced a shock and turned to stare. Could it be *he*? No, impossible. *He* would be over sixty now and this man was not much over thirty. No wonder there was such a resemblance. The visitor was the Emperor's nephew.

In many Louisiana homes a crudely colored picture was piously kept on the mantel. It represented Napoleon among a group of children. The oldest one, erect and elegant in his small uniform of *chasseur de la Garde*, a blond strand of hair across his forehead, was Achille Murat, son of the dashing cavalry officer Joachim Murat, husband of Caroline Bonaparte and, for a while, King of Naples. When the Bourbons' return cost Murat his kingdom and his life, his wife and four children moved to Austria. After a few years, Achille left for the United States to visit his Uncle Joseph. In 1826 New Orleans papers announced that Prince Murat had married a young widow he met in Florida, a great-grandniece of George Washington.

Having become a gentleman farmer in Florida, Achille briefly visited New Orleans. He must have liked this "Western Babylon," as he called the great port, evidently with more curiosity than contempt. After a trip to Europe and another stay in Florida, he decided to settle in New Orleans. He did so partly for financial reasons, as his Florida investment had not proved successful. Would it not be more profitable to acquire land in Mexico, whose Texan part touched Louisiana? The Count de Survilliers might have suggested this; frequently he had heard Lakanal speak about this part of the continent.

In the meantime, the Prince became an American citizen, "read law" as the expression went, and passed the bar examination. In January, 1837 the *Abeille* announced that "Achille Murat and Alexandre Servant, attorneys, are opening their office in Exchange Alley, three doors from café Ambrogio." In changing nationality, Murat had abandoned his title. This would also make him less distant from the type of clients he was going to advise. When General Garrigues de Flaugeac came to pay his respects to his former chief's son, he must have encountered Mexicans who had been persuaded by agents to sell their portions of land.

When the business day was over, Achille Murat would leave the narrow Exchange Alley with its odor of frying food which reminded him of Naples, and return to his residence on the aristocratic Esplanade. He and his wife had rented a mansion there and entertained frequently in its ornate parlors. With their double ascendance from Bonaparte and Washington, the Murats should have been favorites in both Creole and American societies. Yet, they were not. Perhaps Achille, who discussed philosophy in his correspondence with Ralph Waldo Emerson, was too serious to take part in the gay bantering and repartee of New Orleans salons so reminiscent of *Ancien Régime* France. Perhaps also the crow stew, slices of alligators and boiled owls the eccentric host served to his dinner guests was too distasteful to the average person.

If we had a Murat heading the cavalry corps of our Legion, what fame it would bring us, some Frenchmen must have thought. No doubt, Colonel Jean Baptiste Benjamin Vignié would have gladly yielded his place to such an eminent person. Vignié had no need to fear. This son of glamorous Joachim showed no interest in military ranks or brilliant uniforms; in fact, he gave little attention to veterans who had served his family.

Therefore there was little regret when the Murats moved to Baton Rouge. They settled on an estate called Magnolia Mound, but later returned to Florida, the area of the South they preferred. They were buried near Tallahassee.

There was a Murat Street in New Orleans, and it found itself in good company among Alexander and Solomon Streets and a second Napoleon Street. Not far away was Bernadotte Street, glorifying the general who became King of Sweden and married little Désirée Cleary who once had attracted young Bonaparte's attention.

New Orleans was growing. Now public carriages drawn by robust horses took passengers to the deepest convexity of the crescent. Was it under Buisson's influence that an Eagle Street nestled near Cambronne, named for the general whose coarse rebuff to the English demand for surrender at Waterloo had never been forgotten? There was also a street honoring Marshal Ney, "the brave among the brave" who, upon the Bourbons' return, faced the firing squad. Later on a story spread that he had escaped to the United States and was a school teacher in North Carolina. But no inkling of this reached the Louisiana press. One can also find here and there on a New Orleans map names that are reminders of the Napoleonic era: Lannes, Desaix, Stephen Girard. At the very end of the Napoleon Avenue that Buisson had opened, like a little island torn from a continent, is Elba. At home at night when the engineer bent over his plans, he may have been disturbed by young voices daring to ask: "Why not a Waterloo Street?" "Waterloo! Never!" Yet, there was a Waterloo plantation in Louisiana; probably, it belonged to "strangers."

The word "stranger" had become an elastic epithet that native and adopted Orleanians hurled at each other on occasion. When Colonel Vignié, Gally or Buisson vigorously insisted that the Legislature give the Legion more funds and urged citizens to show more zeal "in a country like ours where at any time we may be called to arms," there was always someone to repeat sarcastically: "A country like ours?" To what country did they belong? Once a commander of the militia was bold enough to give an order to the Orleans troops. They refused to obey. Judge Livingston, well known for having been instrumental in the adoption of the *Code Napoléon* in Louisiana, was consulted. He upheld the Orleans Legion's independence.

Supervising an officers' election, Buisson was often aware of discord, but it was not made public unless it resulted in a duel. General Jackson had forbidden duelling among the military and the rule still stood, but Frenchmen and Creoles, true descendants of the men who had defied Richelieu's order at the risk of their lives, ignored that interdiction. One duel was never forgotten.

It was between a German, Lieutenant Schamburg, and the Frenchman, Adolphe Cuvillier. "What weapon do you choose?" Cuvillier had asked. "The sword and on horse back," Schamburg replied.

Cuvillier was familiar with neither sword nor horses. Excited Gallic voices were heard voicing dismay. From his Fontainebleau estate, Mandeville de Marigny heard about the commotion. He had spent three years at St. Cyr as a guest of Louis Philippe, who was thankful for the de Marigny family's help at a time of need. He had become a cavalry lieutenant and had brought back home his love of horses and equestrian skill. An invitation was hastily sent. Each day for a week Cuvillier went to Fontainebleau. His protector had chosen the best horse for that kind of tournament and for hours drilled him in the handling of a sword.

The encounter took place on a racing field uptown. Public cars going to Carrollton emptied load after load of passengers, while the rich came in their barouches or their caleches. The levee was covered with spectators. Others were standing on barges, and seamen had climbed to masts. Thin Adolphe Cuvillier was in complete contrast with herculean Lieutenant Schamburg of the 2nd Dragoons. Some spectators were placing bets, but there was anguish in the air. When the signal was given, Schamburg charged. Cuvillier waited for him leaning forward, and his blade opened a deep gash in the neck of his opponent's horse. Bloody white horse and rider both fell down. "It was a magnificent spectacle!" the French gazettes gloated the next day.

"What are we going to do with all the foreigners who apply to join our Legion?" This question must have often entered the minds of Buisson, Gally and Vignié. It was flattering to see such interest in the Legion, but with

Dr. Antommarchi and Prince Murat

the number of Irish and Anglo-Saxon members increasing, the original group saw their power diminishing. Yet another generation, including the sons of Frederic Buisson and Fleury Generelly, had made its entry into the ranks. Sometimes a newcomer like Louis Surgi, an engineer, was adopted because his father had served the Empire. In another parish, so was Eugene Dumez, who had brought with him from France the memoirs written by his father, Jean Baptiste Dumez, a former *grognard*. But in the New Orleans Legion the problem was more acute. To refuse admission to the "foreigners" was impossible, not only because of democratic principles but because of utilitarian motives. After repeated pressures, the Legislature agreed to vote more funds with the understanding that the Legion should be ready to serve in case of public dangers, and public dangers were frequent.

"What are we going to do with all those foreigners, Commandant?" Commandant Buisson (he now had a title equivalent to major) had an idea. He decided to organize a *Grande Armée*, a conglomeration of corps belonging to different nationalities. Each would choose its own officers, its uniforms, its banners. By right of priority, Creoles and French would be at the head of any military display in this order: Benjamin Buisson's Cannoneers, Vignié's Cuirassiers, Gally's Infantrymen. Then would follow the American Washington Artillery, the German Jaegers, the Italian Carabinieri, the Spanish Cazadores, and the Irish Montgomery Guards. Only the Egyptian Mamelucks were lacking in that miniature Great Army, commented veterans who had named their town Mansura.*

* Mansura, in Northwest Louisiana, was said to have been named after the site of a battle in Bonaparte's Egyptian campaign.

One of these elements, the Washington Guards, caused difficulties. They were recruited almost exclusively from the uptown section. They refused to go down to the Place d'Armes for drills or parades. The distance was not the cause of the discord, but to rendezvous (the English part of the newspapers loved that made-up verb) there meant a recognition of French supremacy. On a Fourth of July, the storm broke. As a conciliatory gesture, a brigadier general had selected a meeting place outside of the city gates. Three Creole officers bristled. The *Advertiser*, the voice of the American public, and the *Courrier de la Louisiane*, faithfully French, joined the fight. Excited men invaded the *Advertiser* office and kidnapped the journalist accused of having insulted their regiment. Realizing they had the wrong man, but without taking time to release him, they started on a new and successful hunt for the culprit. Frightened passers-by called the police. The victim was locked in the Calaboose for protection. "Everything is quiet," the *Courrier* briefly stated the next day. To avoid a longer jail term, the journalist offered his apologies. The French Legionnaires were jubilant. They had won another victory.

Not long before, they had demonstrated their power. Comrade Bernard Bourdin, formerly of the San Domingo expedition and for a while one of the Gulf buccaneers, had a son who committed suicide. A religious funeral was denied him. Armed Legionnaires entered the Presbytery. They were not very pious, but for three occasions they needed the clergy: baptism, marriage and death. Young Bourdin would have black-cassocked priests around his coffin even if they had to be brought by force!

The men could find some satisfaction for their bellicose feelings in maneuvers. These were so like real war that sometimes Dr. Yves Le Monnier had to be called. He was a Breton, former member of the troops sent by Bonaparte to the West Indies and now the Legion's Head Surgeon. The mock fights ended in noisy banquets. All this may have seemed childish to visitors, but the regiments had their usefulness. One day, during the course of a ceremony, ladies offered Commandant Buisson a flag they had embroidered "as a token of gratitude for having extinguished a revolt which might have proved dangerous." What revolt? Local newspapers remained silent, just as earlier they had ignored a dramatic event reported only in Buisson's *Courrier de Nachitoches*: the invasion of the Collège d'Orléans by rioting blacks.

XI

The Napoleonic Legend in Louisiana Poetry

SPRING WAS TOO SHORT. After masked balls and Mardi Gras parades, a custom probably introduced by students returning home from Paris, came the sinister procession of tumbrels carting corpses away. It was like an Orcagna's fresco on which brilliant young knights come face to face with skeletons.

Reverend Theodore Clapp of the First Presbyterian Church, along with other ministers and a handful of Roman Catholic priests, hastened from house to house bringing spiritual comfort to yellow fever victims. On one occasion Reverend Clapp entered a stuffy room, raised the mosquito bar and heard a voice which unexpectedly asked: "What do you think of Napoleon's character?" A few hours later, the clergyman returned and, bending close to the dying man's swollen lips, asked what his last wish was. "Pray that in the celestial regions I may enjoy the sight and the company of the greatest and best man who ever lived, the Emperor Napoleon."

After he went back to New England, Reverend Clapp related this incident in the book he wrote about his thirty years of ministry in the Deep South. He identified the man only by saying that he had turned his home into a museum of Imperial souvenirs. This could apply to former mayor Nicholas Girod. Or could it have been Pierre Caillou, the exuberant Gascon? Other names come to mind. The year was not mentioned and the fact that there was an epidemic is not revealing. If a period had to be chosen to locate this scene, the decade 1840–50 would be most appropriate. The transformation of Napoleon into a legendary hero had reached its zenith.

"Everybody wishes that Napoleon's body be returned to France," Pierre Cherbonnier had written in his *Alphabet*. King Louis Philippe decided it was time to satisfy public opinion by respecting the St. Helena prisoner's last desire: "I wish that my body rest on the banks of the Seine among the French people I have loved so much." England had accepted the suggestion. It was less costly than making some concession in the ever-recurrent Middle East crisis.

As soon as the news reached the United States, the New Orleans reading-rooms, well-stacked with local gazettes as well as papers from New York, Boston, Philadelphia and Baltimore, were thronged by the exiles. The word "exiles" might well have applied once again since, as the veterans read of the preparations being made in Paris, their eyes became misty. They would not be present to salute their *Petit Caporal*.

"We are several old soldiers of the Empire who have exchanged swords for ploughs and the tumult of camp life for the peaceful retreats of the Mississippi shores." Thus began a letter sent from the Acadian country in Southern Louisiana to the *Abeille de la Nouvelle Orléans*. Amid the gratitude expressed to the King one criticism appeared. Why send only a frigate with such a ridiculous name, *La Belle Poule* (The Beautiful Hen), when a whole fleet would not have been too much?

In New Orleans an appeal was sent to all Frenchmen,

"naturalized or not." A big ceremony was to take place as soon as the news of the Paris celebration arrived. The Napoleonic enthusiasm had spread among the Americans for other reasons. England menacingly looked at the United States' advance toward Mexico, and toward the Texas frontier also went many Louisianians' aspirations. Therefore, for political as well as sentimental motives, anti-British feelings were widely expressed. This produced a revival of the atmosphere that had been known at the beginning of the century.

To a greater extent even than in 1821, as newspapers were more numerous and larger, articles about the Imperial era appeared daily in the Louisiana press. Out in the parishes veterans provided anecdotes. In Alexandria, in the central part of the state, a Lutheran minister announced that he would speak three times a week, by candlelight, *"du caractère, des moeurs et des manières de l'Empereur Napoléon et de sa femme Joséphine"* (about Napoleon and Josephine's characters, morals and manners). This preacher who gave such a large share to Caesar in God's temple was J. J. Lehmanowsky, born in Warsaw, a former colonel of a Polish regiment which was part of the *Grande Armée*. According to his own story he had been sentenced by Louis XVIII to be executed one day after his chief, Marshal Ney. A certain countess sent him a cake containing a steel file. He sawed through the iron bars and let himself down with a rope made of bed clothes. A sentinel who recognized him let him pass. Lehmanowsky was sure that Ney also had escaped to America.

"Beautiful as glory, cold as a tomb," said **Victor** Hugo of the funeral day in Paris. It took over two months for the full description to reach New Orleans. One learned that 400 women had worked for weeks to make black and silver draperies, that dignitaries of all nations except England had attended the service. What else could one have expected from Albion? Louisianians were too far away to have heard of unpleasant details: the bourgeois King's pettiness, his son Joinville's resentment at having been chosen for what he called an undertaker's role. The worst of it was the interruption of his affair with an opera dancer that the Parisians quickly nicknamed *La Belle Poule.*

Hotel St. Louis was a large and stately building containing a stock exchange, a hotel, and rooms for auction sales or meetings. Its dominating feature was its great dome. There, on January 10 at eleven o'clock, *"heure militaire,"* as the *Courrier de la Louisiane* had said, a group of veterans gathered to plan a ceremony. The French Consul won the ex-soldiers' hearts when he refused the Presidency of the Committee: "Someone who had served under *him* should preside." The men looked at each other, and decided to vote. Unanimously, Benjamin Buisson was elected. There seemed to be no resentment over the fact that he had abandoned the old quarter and had moved pioneer-like to the new section.

The Frenchmen were adopting the American custom of forming committees and subcommittees. They were needed to take care of all the gifts. Not only money was offered. A carpenter donated the wood and the hours of work required for the building of a cenotaph. Monsignor Blanc, the archbishop, would officiate at a pontifical Mass for the repose of the Emperor's soul. All the Legion corps would assemble as early as seven o'clock on the morning of March 21. The newspapers printed a vignette showing the uniforms the Jaegers, the Carabinieri and others would wear. An imposing force of ushers was selected. Wearing a wide crape band on their left arms, they would carefully check the invitations at the gates of St. Louis Cathedral. This last detail was the spark that ignited the fire.

On the morning of January 21, the gazettes announced that the funeral service had been cancelled. The city was in an uproar. To be deprived of a procession and a grandiose ceremony was unthinkable. What had happened? "All Christians—or rather all inhabitants of the city—have the right to enter a church," the wardens had stated, and for twenty years or more the wardens' word was the law. The ushers declared that they would follow the orders they had received. Attempts at mediation were rejected. Boiling with rage, Buisson had to announce the final decision. His Imperial Majesty would have to do without a Mass, but his soldiers would not yield their positions. Referring to the elaborate preparations which had come to naught, a newspaper editor commented that it was like the fable of the mountain giving birth to a mouse.

What was the real cause of that fiasco? Were the wardens so pious or so democratic that they could not stand the idea of a church being closed for an hour to uninvited persons? It is more likely that their attitude had come from a smothering hostility toward the Frenchmen. A month earlier the Native American Party, which soon would be called only the American Party, had held a convention in New Orleans. The members were opposed to Irish and German immigrants, but also to Catholics. Many of the Napoleonic exiles were Free Masons, but officially they belonged to the Roman Catholic Church and for this reason were distrusted by the Native Americans. The disagreement about the funeral Mass furnished an opportunity to stir up dissension among the Catholics. "Are you going to take orders from foreigners?" the wardens asked. The veterans had been defeated. They were losing face.

It had been a fad among local poets to offer Napoleon's *grognards* as examples of patriotic virtues. Such praises went to some heads, among them Prosper Foy's. Bordeaux and St. Domingue may have contributed to his fiery imagination. Neither the care of his plantation nor his childless home were enough to occupy his time. He supplied a local review, *Le Bon Sens*, with poems and songs in which the usual refrain was: "*Napoleon, la patrie et l'honneur!*" On his frequent visits to New Orleans he would bring *l'Abeille* articles. One of them caused a violent storm. Boldly, Prosper Foy had stated that on the Chalmette battlefield some American officers, "with an utter disregard for the laws of war," had given the order to shoot at a messenger sent by the enemy. Luckily, according to the author, a chivalrous Frenchman, Major de St. Gème, ran to General Jackson and reminded him that an emissary's rights are sacred.

Whether the incident had really happened could not be ascertained, but Foy's *faux pas* started a polemic that did not benefit the veterans. Occurring only a month before the planned ceremony, it must have been partly responsible for its failure. Strangely enough, it did not affect the growing enthusiasm for the Emperor's memory. On March 21, 1840 the cenotaph built by the devoted carpenter Giraudon remained without mourners, but the Orleanians expressed their feelings in another way. The Orleans Theater showed a drama in five tableaux, *Napoléon à St. Hélène*, while at the American Theater the popular actor Conner played the main part in *Napoleon ou Vive l'Empereur*. Both spectacles ended with the singing of the *Marseillaise*. On that day, St. Louis Cathedral's organ remained silent, but *L'Abeille* published twenty-four stanzas written by Victor de Bouchelle. In this ode to *Le Guerrier Intrépide* (The Intrepid Warrior), the prolific Creole poet placed Napoleon above the giants of all centuries, including *"le Vieil Adamastor"* (The Old Adamastor).

In the middle of the 19th century, a group of French-speaking men devoted their leisure hours to literary pursuits and furnished enough material to keep several publishing firms busy. Through them the Napoleonic legend was in full poetic flight. In spite of some verbal skirmishes in the past, the veterans were still objects of praise. The Creole Dominique Rouquette offered Maurice Barnett and his comrades as an example of courage: *"Ainsi que Barnett à Chalmette, Doux agneaux changés en lions."* (Like Barnett at Chalmette, Gentle lambs changed into lions.) Dominique remembered the time when he and his brother Adrien, the future missionary, invited Choctaws to form a circle around them and described the exploits of the Great Mingo (chief). This French warrior had fought the Battle of the Sand (Egypt), the Battle of the Sun (Austerlitz) and the Battle of the Snows (Russia).

Tullius de St. Céran, born in Jamaica but educated at the Collège d'Orléans, recalled the Napoleonic soldiers' share in the victory of 1815. It seemed a premonition of Waterloo; they wanted to avenge it. This same Tullius de St. Céran had declared that "every Creole is a poet." In this circle of mutual admiration, however, some Frenchmen from France were admitted. There were Guillaume Montmain, still active, Urbain David, who did not fail to follow his signature with "de Cette" as he did not want his native town to be forgotten, and others.

The most picturesque among them probably was Constant Lepouzé. Arriving in America as a *demi-solde*, he still longed for the day he could afford to go back home. Unfortunately, neither translating Horace nor giving lessons proved profitable enough. Even as a young man he looked like the typical old school teacher of that era. No one had ever seen him without a ruler in one hand and a snuff box in the other. A judge once made a sarcastic remark about the Collège d'Orléans, and Lepouzé felt that his honor commanded him to fight a duel. For the occasion he left his ruler behind, but not his snuff box. Just before the seconds gave the starting signal, Lepouzé offered a pinch of tobacco to his adversary, who burst out laughing. No blood was shed.

The *Gazette des Opelousas* revealed another poet who signed his work as S. Bernard. Antoine Blanc and H. Germain, who had opened the Lycée de Baton Rouge, were also literary contributors. H. Germain probably was the Henri Germain whose name had been on the list of Champ d'Asile's refugees. Unless a detail such as the one mentioned about Germain attracts attention, it was difficult to tell whether a writer lived on the banks of the Seine or of the Mississippi. There is an almost complete absence of local color. A classical influence lingered, sprinkling nymphs and zephyrs through pompous lines. As to the contemporary great or less great men of Paris, only two were recognized as masters: Hugo and Béranger. The taste had not changed between the 1820s and the 1840s.

St. Céran called the leader of the Romantic school his "handsome knight" and, in an image which would have delighted Hugo himself, compared him to Niagara Falls. He closely imitated even his technique. Placide Canonage, son of the Judge Canonge who spoke at Napoleon's funeral service in 1821 and who dabbled in drama, was one of the most ardent *hugolâtres*. He grouped his friends around him to read them scenes from *Hernani* and *Ruy Blas*, and one could not be sure whether he was applauding Canonge or his great model.

Boismare's cases of books had ceased circulating on the bayous, but there were other ways to keep in touch with the literary production. Often travelers gave away or sold reading matter they had brought with them. A discovery would circulate among friends, reaching a gazette editor. Thus Hugo's *"Sire, vous rentrerez dans votre capitale"* (Sire, you will return to your capital) was reproduced not only in the *Courrier de la Louisiane* but in the *Gazette de Baton Rouge* and in another small sheet printed in the Attakapas section. In his diary the planter Ferry, between the price received for sugarcane and the fact that little Alexis had cried when leaving for a boarding school, had copied in his clearest handwriting: *"Sire, vous rentrerez dans votre capitale."* In her album bound in rose velvet, between two pressed flowers, a young girl had written in purple ink: *"Sire, vous rentrerez...."*

However popular Victor Hugo was in New Orleans, he could hardly reach the pedestal on which Béranger stood. When St. Céran heard that the bard's political opinions might lead him into trouble, in a vibrant ode he invited him to come to the banks of the Mississippi. When Constant Lepouzé wanted to praise St. Céran, he could not find a better compliment than to make the Meschacebé boast to the Seine: "I also have my Béranger!" Poor Alexandre Latil, from Lepers' land where a terrible disease had relegated him, lamented the fact that Béranger had not been elected to the French Academy. Charles Testut, a Creole, spoke of the "shivers and gold dreams" the name of Béranger stirred in his heart. A club, Les Amis de Béranger, was organized. Returning from Paris, Dominique Rouquette proudly told his friends

The Napoleonic Legend in Louisiana Poetry 167

that Béranger teasingly had called him "my young savage." To be the great man's young savage was indeed an honor. An old musician of the Orleans Theater who boasted he had played before Czar Alexander and Napoleon kept among his most precious mementoes a ring on which an eagle was engraved and a few lines Béranger had asked him to set to music. *Harper's Weekly* of February 26, 1859 recorded his death in New Orleans, saying: "He had occupied a distinguished place among the musicians of one of Napoleon's military bands and his execution had frequently attracted attention from the Great Man himself."

Hugo and Béranger were the great favorites less because of their literary merits than because they were considered as being the high priests of the Napoleonic cult. In the prolific spring of 1841, poems scattered here and there were considered not enough to satisfy the public. The *Courrier de la Louisiane* asked its readers to subscribe to the publication of a volume of verses called *Les Impériales*. Its author, Auguste Lussan, a Parisian actor, carefully let it be known in his preface that his father, an old soldier, was ending his life at the Invalides, near the Emperor's tomb. Preface, subject matter and technique were bound to attract success.

When the agitation brought forth by the return of the Emperor's remains to Paris was about to diminish, an event revived it. Marshal Bertrand* and his son Napoleon were coming to New Orleans. Louisianians, anxious to find out what was bringing them, learned that Mrs. Bertrand had inherited properties in Martinique. In 1836 she died. Her husband took a trip to the Antilles with his son Arthur. They enjoyed hunting so much that they

---

* Marshal Bertrand and his family stayed at St. Helena until the Emperor's death.

remained for two years on their estate, Les Salines. In 1842 Bertrand decided to return, this time with another of his children, Napoleon's godson. He became interested in the slavery question and wished to study it in other parts of the world.

The "faithful among the faithful" was about to land. Again the city would offer gun salutes, speeches, banquets. At night both the French Quarter and the business section displayed transparencies announcing "greetings to our illustrious guests." The crowd stood under the visitors' windows of the newly built St. Charles Hotel. The applause was thunderous. The following day newspapers reported that in the course of a reception the Marshal had recognized Messieurs Buisson, Barnett and Mercier. Had Bertrand acquired that uncanny talent to remember faces through Bonaparte's contact or had someone at the St. Charles' prompted him?

It is said that one veteran failed to reach his former chief. He had lived for many years as a recluse several miles from New Orleans. When he arrived, dazzled by the lights and deafened by the tumult, he was unable to find his way and, sadly, returned to his faraway shack. No name was mentioned. One may surmise that this hermit was the former Royal Street bric-a-brac and art dealer Antoine Michoud.

The Bertrands could not stay long in Louisiana, yet they could not refuse to travel on the little railroad engineered by Colonel Claudius Crozet. At the Milneburg station a reception committee was waiting for them. What touched Bertrand's heart far more than bands and banners was the sight of an humble fisherman fighting his way through dignitaries. In a burst of emotion which delighted the audience, the *Grand Maréchal* and his *grognard* embraced.

The Napoleonic Legend in Louisiana Poetry 169

Napoleon's cult was turning to fanaticism. It was as dangerous to get embroiled in a political discussion if one felt lukewarm toward the Imperial regime as it was to belittle the public's favorite prima donna. Elie Deron, former graduate of Paris' Ecole des Chartes, taught at the pension for *jeunes demoiselles* opened by his wife. His fellow countryman, Armand Gareau, was also a professor there. The strong friendship between Deron and Gareau dramatically came to an end when in one of his poems Deron placed Washington above any other great man. Peace was restored only when Deron preferred not to reply to an apostrophe addressed by Gareau to his hero: "Who would dare to challenge you in your Pantheon?" A similar quarrel burst out between Tullius de St. Céran, who had become one of Washington's great admirers, and Charles Testut, author of a volume of verses, *Feuilles d'Été (Summer Leaves)*, reminiscent of Hugo's *Feuilles d'Automme.*

Any form of activity exercised an influence upon Louisiana. Scientific minds were stimulated by young Leverrier's discovery of a new planet, Neptune. This revived the interest that Benjamin Buisson had shown for astronomy in his student days. Perhaps also he had more leisure and the house was quieter now that the children had grown. In 1849 he published *Des Forces qui Régissent le Système Solaire* (Forces which Rule the Solar System), explaining his goal thus: "First, I intend to study the principal causes of gravitation, secondly the force which pushes the system from West to East, thirdly, the cause of this movement." He intended to follow Descartes' Method in the treatment of his problems. He avoided the flowery style so popular at that time saying: "There are subjects so majestic that ornamentation would appear superfluous." He ended with a philosophical remark: "Astronomy has been blamed for lowering the human race by enlarging the Universe and reducing the Earth to a speck in the immensity, but Science which elevates our ideas so high shows us that man's importance is to be measured neither by the space he occupies nor the size of the globe where he makes his habitat." In the course of his treatise, the versatile man found opportunities to praise Laplace, Leverrier and other French scientists. Benjamin Buisson was paying tribute to France while studying the stars.

"If ever a call to arms was heard on our shores, the Orleans Battalion would return to the city only after having covered itself with laurels." Thus spoke Benjamin Buisson the day the Governor officially had placed into his hands the battalion's azure and gold banner.

Had the moment come when this promise must be kept? Many years had passed since unruly General Humbert, acting as a condottiere, had become embroiled in Mexican intrigues. Texas was now a republic, on friendly terms with Louisiana. However, Mexico refused to relinquish its claim on it. Property owners on the Eastern bank of the Sabine River felt threatened. Punitive expeditions were urged by the press. General Zachary Taylor, in charge of defending Texas against Mexican aggressors, requested General Gaines, quartered in New Orleans, to furnish him well-trained artillerymen. The Legionnaires volunteered their service, as did the Native Americans. Both companies were placed under the command of Louis Gally. How proud he must have felt! Perhaps personal problems kept Benjamin Buisson at home. In spite of his sixty years, when Gally marched toward the harbor at the head of his men, he was as erect as the tall lieutenant who had arrived in the city many years before. Amidst the crowd's acclamations, the troops boarded the *Alabama*. For three months, they would furnish help to General Taylor.

The following year, 1846, Taylor again found himself dangerously surrounded by Mexicans and called for help. Once more Louis Gally and his regiment answered the call. This time they experienced disappointment. They were assigned to guard the forts along the Mississippi River, replacing regular soldiers sent to fight. Mosquito bites were nothing compared to their wounded pride. Is the city going to make fun of us at the next Fourth of July parade, they wondered sadly? On the contrary, Orleanians sympathized with them and even helped some of the volunteers who, upon their return, found themselves financially embarrassed. When regular regiments returned from Mexico, Gally and his artillery corps occupied a place of honor, and the Legion added to its calendar a new feast, that of St. Louis.

About the time of Gally's first expedition, the Legion lost one of its most faithful members, Charles Cuvelier, who had received from the men under his command many tokens of esteem, among them a sword and a gold snuff box. For a quarter of a century, he had been the Director of Milne's Home for Destitute Boys, a position which brought him much prestige and very little money. "He was honest, he died poor," the *Courrier de la Nouvelle Orléans* wrote in his obituary. The whole city mourned the kind-hearted, dignified Lorrain. Guillaume Montmain, still active, wrote an ode to the memory of the man who "fought twenty years for his beloved France and for twenty more years served and cherished his new country." As Orleanians sang even when they were sad, Montmain suggested that his verses should be put to the tune of Béranger's *"Nous combations sous les mêmes drapeaux."* (We were fighting under the same flags.)

In the same year, 1845, that Cuvelier died, the State Militia, which for the parishes was the Legion's counterpart, also lost one of its leaders. In spite of the stifling June heat, rich whites, poor whites, Negroes and Indians answered St. Landry's bells tolling for Garrigues de Flaugeac's funeral. All the villagers knew they had lost a man who had taken care of their interests in the Senate for eighteen years; who was the Brigadier General of their militia; a planter who, without asking for any return, opened his barns wide along Bayou Courtableau to farmers' products waiting for barges. Desirous to improve the health of the inhabitants, he had sent for his nephew, Dr. de Roaldes, who arrived from Southern France and settled in Louisiana.

People whispered that probably the dead man was not going to leave his family as wealthy as could have been expected. He was too fond of helping people and often, in a generous gesture, he ignored the hand offering a receipt for money lent to a friend, a neighbor or simply anyone in need. How many of these debtors would come forward to repay their heirs? Apparently not many did, since everything had to be sold: Prairie Plaisance, Bayou Boeuf, horses and caleche. In the inventory—a pell-mell listing of the silverware, the maple armoire and the tools— a few slaves were listed, each with his value and his shortcoming: one-legged Jeudi, fifty dollars; Spry, afflicted with a hernia, three hundred dollars; and 75 year-old Marinette, only five dollars. Luckily, Mrs. de Flaugeac, née Marie Louise Fontenot, who still signed with a cross, was able to buy back a good part of the estate; luckily also her son had returned from Europe, his law studies ended. With less grandeur than his father but with a pleasing equanimity, Judge Garrigues, as he became, continued to be one of the leading spirits of the community as for centuries the Flaugeacs had been in their chateau overlooking the Lot River in Southern France.

In the St. Landry cemetery of Opelousas Parish, on a slab held above the ground by six columns, an inscription to the memory of Antoine Garrigues de Flaugeac was engraved:

> "*Volontaire de l'Armée d'Italie en 1800.*
> (A volunteer in the campaign of Italy of 1800)
>
> *Officier d'infanterie sur les champs de bataille de St. Domingue.*
> (Infantry officer on the battlefields of St. Domingue)
>
> *Fils adoptif de l'Union, il se couvrit de glorie dans cette immortelle campagne de 1814–1815 qui la délivra pour toujours du joug de la fière Albion.*
> (Adopted son of the Union, he covered himself with glory in that immortal campaign 1814–1815, which forever delivered it from proud Albion's supremacy.)
>
> *Législateur vertueux et éclairé, il emporte les regrets de tous les bons citoyens.*"
> (A virtuous and enlightened legislator, he died mourned by all good citizens.)

XII

Their Last War

"As sudden and as rapid as a thunderbolt news of a bloody revolution in Paris arrived stirring up the most intense surprise and anxiety," the *Abeille* announced on March 25, 1848. During the following weeks, two or three pages of the four pages of each issue of the *Courrier de la Nouvelle Orléans* and the *Abeille* commented in English and French on Louis Philippe's fall. Louisianians heard that Paris once more had erected barricades, and that demonstrators almost had adopted a red flag when Lamartine reminded them that their tricolor had toured the world "with your liberties and your glories." This dramatic statement was sure to find an echo, and Lamartine as a deputy met with more favor than he had had as a poet.

Democratic America exulted to see another republic being born. The new French regime had been proclaimed on February 22, Washington's birthday, and this appeared as a good omen. For a while, attention turned away from Mexican affairs and presidential elections. One day, however, the United States' interior policy became involved with the Parisian events. In New York big posters had appeared on walls bearing the words, "French Republic, Democratic Whig Nomination for President, George Washington Lafayette." New Orleans did not know how serious this declaration was, but young Lafayette's visit with his father was remembered, and the French group was flattered by that thought.

The enthusiasm which greeted Louis Philippe I when he replaced Charles X and the gratitude expressed when he had Napoleon's remains transferred to the Invalides were now forgotten. In a dramatic appeal, the *Abeille* expressed the hope that the movement started in Paris would spread all over Europe, "to Switzerland and among pikes and precipices inspire new William Tells, that it would reach Italian plains and encourage the degenerate children of this sunny land to follow their heroic ancestors' examples, that it would wake up enslaved and tortured Ireland and would break the chains with which Austria had encircled five million human beings."

In New Orleans the Italian brethren of those "degenerate children" did not resent this epithet and organized meetings and parades. Naturally, the greatest part in the demonstrations should belong to people with French blood, and they answered this invitation with their usual vim. Two banquets were planned. To attend one would cost one dollar the other two dollars. A hue and cry went up. Was it logical to celebrate the triumph of equality and fraternity by separating the poor from the rich? Made uneasy by this rebuke, the hospitality committee had the newspapers announce that anyone would be welcome whether he paid or not. It was not surprising that 700 persons met for a "sumptuous repast" in the favorite open-air restaurant, "The Rock of St. Helena's Garden." Between courses, people at one table, then another, began singing, and everyone joined in for the refrain: *"Napoléon, la patrie et l'honneur!"*

Parishes followed the example set by the city, and they also addressed their congratulations to the leaders of the new Republic, who, no doubt were astonished to receive official letters from places with names as exotic as Catahoula, Ouachita and Natchitoches. The veterans who, as Victor Hugo might have said, were entering their *"vieillesse conteuse,"* (their reminiscing old age), did not let anyone forget that *they* had carried the tricolor through Europe. Victor Cherbonnier, now superintendent of the Donaldsonville school system, saw to it that *Le Vigilant* was well supplied with anecdotes about the France he had served, and Lafargue in his *Villageois* and other ex-soldiers through other gazettes did the same.

In the course of all the festivities, Pierre Soulé, who later would become United States Ambassador to Spain, made a strange remark for a man born in the cheerful Midi. He accused his fellow countrymen of not being "serious enough." Whether he succeeded in calming their exuberance remains doubtful.

About that time, the Native Americans, less an organized party than an influence whose weight was increasing, attracted attention to the right to vote that was too quickly granted to newcomers. The Frenchmen who had grown roots in Louisiana also were watching with reluctance the influx of Italians, Germans and Irishmen. One of the Presidential candidates was General Zachary Taylor of Louisiana. French veterans liked him because he had acknowledged the aid of Louis Gally and the Legion. His candidacy was upheld by the Whigs who in turn received the Native Americans' help. French and Americans were therefore united against newcomers.

All this political agitation seemed to have gone to the head of an ex-captain of the Imperial Army named Dugarry. A meeting was to be held on the levee. Dugarry, who should have been tamed by his many years as an humble office worker, appeared brandishing a sword. In a frenzy, he rushed up to a group of petrified Irishmen and stabbed a young man. The victim's friends seized stones, shells and pieces of wood, all the projectiles the floatsam furnished, and hurled them at Dugarry, killing him. That night in the Third District, where immigrants had built narrow houses hugging each other, the population went en masse to the Irish wake. In the French Quarter a well-known Creole named de Buys had opened his home to Dugarry's body. Dismayed by the tragedy, Buisson, Gally, Barnett, Courcelle and Dominique de Castelnau stood guard around their dead comrade.

"I came back from exile to place myself under the new Republic's flag, my only ambition being to serve my country. I am announcing my arrival to the members of the Provisory Government." Thus Louis Napoleon Bonaparte wrote a few days after Louis Philippe I had fallen from power. The *Abeille* reproduced the letter and followed it with a brief commentary: "The prince was requested to remain away from France a little longer."

In the preceding years the two clumsy attempts that Napoleon's nephew, son of King Louis of Holland and Queen Hortense, Josephine's daughter, had made to excite French opinion in his favor had hardly attracted the attention of the Louisiana press. Yet, it would have been expected that Orleanians would have doubly cherished a descendant of the Bonapartes and the Beauharnais. This dreamy man with his long waxed moustache bore too little resemblance to his dynamic Corsican uncle.

"Celui qui maintenant repose aux Invalides Ne peut
  avoir de successeur"
(The one who now rests at the
Invalides
Cannot have a successor.)

Urbain David's verses actually reflected New Orleans' general opinion. Therefore Louis Napoleon's coup d'etat on the very anniversary of the Coronation and the Austerlitz victory provoked violent indignation. "Terror reigns . . . Two thousand men killed . . . Victor Hugo in flight..." Such were the broad headlines.

The sensational piece of news had arrived just at the moment of the celebration of the battle of January 8, 1815, as now the time elapsed between European events and their echoes in America had shrunk to about five weeks. Writing about the *Marseillaise* to be sung at the opera the night of January 8, the gazettes commented: "For a few spectators it will be a magnificent memory, for others it will be the most energetic protestation in favor of the Republic." The city where *fleur de lys* formerly had been broken in favor of eagles now was refusing to place faith in one Napoleon while still adoring the other. Later on when it became official that the Empire had been reestablished the Frenchmen from France did not manifest any joy. "Are you going back to France?" veterans were asked. The answer in most cases was a vigorous "No, a thousand times no, if *l'Autre*, the Other, had come back alive from St. Helena, nothing would have kept me from going to serve him . . . but for this one . . ." And shoulders would be shrugged with contempt.

There were a few exceptions to this mood. Dr. Doussan declared that he was leaving for Paris. He wanted to view the Coronation. He was probably disappointed if he had expected to see a new Caesar placing the crown on his own imperial head. Pope Pius IX would not play any part in a ceremony subdued enough not to give any impetus to a widespread hostile current. Yet, the old physician must have heard a *Te Deum* at Notre Dame or witnessed some ceremony, for after his return he wrote to the Emperor: "It was a very beautiful day for him [Doussan] to see your cherished dynasty come to life again, the dynasty of someone so beloved that he [Doussan] still keeps the regreat not to have been granted the favor to go to St. Helena to care for the exile."

A voice more powerful than the good doctor's was heard in Louisiana furiously protesting the Republic's demise. *Napoleon le Petit,* published by Victor Hugo in Brussels, had promptly been reproduced by the *Courrier de la Nouvelle Orléans. Les Châtiments,* in which this same poet gave free rein to his love for antithesis, glorified Napoleon I and reviled Napoleon III.

The poems stirred memories. For one veteran, it recalled his Russian campaign. "After a white plain another white plain. . ." For someone else, it was his last battle: "Waterloo, Waterloo. . ."

The vivid interest for Hugo's virulent satire might have been intensified also by a new factor. The coup d'etat of 1851 had brought to America a fresh wave of exiles. They found in Louisiana the proper ground for spreading their ideas in their own language. Cleverly, they borrowed items from Paris newspapers and, free from any censure, slanted them according to their resentment.

Empire means peace, Louis Napoleon had stated. On the contrary, wars were going to start many times. The local press remarked that the siege of Sebastopol had killed more men through disease alone than the San Domingo expedition and twenty Louisiana summers.

A gesture of the sovereign, however, rallied to his cause some of his former opponents. The Imperial Prince's birth had brought to the fore the urgency of strengthening the dynasty. If only uncle and nephew could be linked together in popular imagination. From this desire was created the St. Helena medal. It would be sent to all the men who had fought between 1792 and 1815. Many of those bronze profiles reached Louisiana and remained among family treasures. Benjamin Buisson opened the little red leather case with sadness. His wife Sophie, who would have shared his emotion, had died. The six children respectfully read the engraved words: "To my companions of glory my last thought." It was another tangible proof that their father had shared in the heroic adventure.

In spite of their gratitude for this gesture by Napoleon III, the veterans could not refrain from thinking that the nephew did not reign well. A visitor to the bloody Italian battlefields of the Austrian campaign, so bloody that the French sovereign shrank from their sight, arrived in New Orleans. He was young Formento who, following in his father's footsteps, had gone to Europe to study medicine. At Magenta and at Solferine he cared for the wounded. Then he decided to return home. In the meantime the older Dr. Felix Formento had not been able to resist a desire to end his life where his childhood had been spent. While he was sailing toward Europe, the young surgeon was crossing the ocean in the opposite direction. When he arrived in New Orleans, the two tall glass jars, one blue, one red, in the window of the apothecary's shop no longer threw their reflection on the Royal Street banquette. The pharmacy, for so long one of the favorite meeting places of the Frenchmen, was closed. Closed also was the tall home on Esplanade. Another Dr. Formento was going to stay in the South, foreseeing perhaps that his services would soon be needed as badly as they had been on European battlefields.

When the American Civil War broke out, few of the Napoleonic exiles were still alive. Yet, some of them, after years in a climate that seemed to have immunized them against fevers, were entering a robust old age. Tall Louis Gally was still erect and his step was brisk, too brisk. Once, hearing a military band, he rushed to the window. His forehead struck the framework and he died a few days later. The Legion escorted his coffin to St. Louis Cemetery as it had also accompanied those of Montmain, the song-writer; Frederic Buisson, the sheriff; Colonel Vignié, the banker; Fleury Generelly, the accountant and artist; and many others.

How would the remaining veterans react when faced with the crisis of the 1860s? When they had left Europe, more than forty years before, race prejudices had no meaning for them. Even if they were not avid readers, they knew that their philosophers had condemned slavery. During their youth, they may have heard about the *Amis des Noirs* (Friends of the Blacks), a group born at the dawn of the French Revolution. Members of the San Domingo expeditionary corps may have observed some unpleasant traits among those "children of nature" of whom 18th century writers spoke with a naive tenderness.

Confusion reigned when the First Consul sent bewildered Marshal Leclerc the order to reestablish slavery. Reestablish slavery when the principles of liberty, equality and fraternity were proclaimed by the French everywhere! "I trust Providence," Toussaint Louverture, the Napoleon of the Blacks, had said with a sardonic smile. Providence was the name of the hospital where hundreds of members of the occupation force were dying every week. Providence was working for the slaves when the great revolutionary ideas had failed.

The Frenchmen who escaped from the Haitian debacle did not keep such a fond memory of the Negroes that they would object to their enslavement. For financial reasons they did without their help for a while. Later on, with or without pangs of conscience, they mingled with Louisianians bidding in the slave market. "In Rome, let us do like the Romans!" they said. Even Lakanal accepted the prevailing view. From Mobile, where he went to live when he left New Orleans, he wrote to the learned Geoffroy St. Hilaire in Paris that he had obtained ten good slaves, promptly adding that he treated them like "unfortunate friends" and required from them only "moderate labor."

Other Frenchmen discreetly, without fanfare, tried to offset unhappy conditions created—who knows?—perhaps by a fellow countryman. Once a young boy was seen running toward the harbor. His dark eyes were filled with tears which rolled down cheeks so pale that anywhere except in New Orleans he could have passed for white.

"Where are you going, Florville?"

"To give papa's letter to the captain of the boat going up the river."

"Why are you crying?"

"Read if you wish."

In a careful, childish handwriting the message sent to a well-known planter said:

"My dear Father,

My hand is trembling. I am hardly able to write. The best friend we had in the whole world has died within five days after an attack of fever...."

"Who taught you how to write?"

"He, who just died, Mr. de Perdreauville. He said that someday I will be able to carve names and dates on tombs. There is always work for that."

So, the former mentor of the Royal and Imperial pages who, during the day taught the *crème de la crème* of the city, at night helped a child doubly handicapped by his illegitimate birth and a few drops of African blood.

"With this so-called air of liberty blowing on our globe and especially in your climate, negroes may try some day to recapture what we have taken from them and will want to be free." This message, mailed from Vaufrey in Eastern France, reached an estate by the same name on the bank of a bayou. But Dr. Monnot, who had baptised his Louisiana property in memory of his childhood home, had died before the warning could reach him. A letter Victor Hugo had sent to Mrs. Chapman, the fiery abolitionist, was translated and printed in Baltimore by one of the Latrobes whose name was so familiar in the South. Latrobe published the letter, not because he approved of it, but, on the contrary, to show that Europeans were not familiar with the different angles of the question. Latrobe's comment carried less weight than Hugo's dramatic declaration: "Barbaric customs in the heart of a society which in itself is a proof of civilisation, liberty wearing a chain, the Negro tied by his neck to Washington's pedestal!"

Veterans of the Napoleonic Wars had fought for revolutionary principles and were Victor Hugo's ardent admirers, but through forty years of residence in the Southern States they could not have remained unaware of color distinction. The conflict was painful. The war broke out. Their sons left to join the Confederate Army, taking with them their fathers' good wishes.

No anniversary of The Battle was ever celebrated with as much solemnity as it was in 1861. Louisiana had just claimed its independence from the United States Government and wanted to display its military qualities. At the head of the long parade came the white and the black men who had fought in 1815. Among them was

Maurice Barnett, a veteran of even older campaigns. Then the Legion followed. Among its ranks may have been a few Napoleonic soldiers but only one was still active enough to have his name recorded in the approaching drama. He was Benjamin Buisson, then sixty-eight years old. Although he had never been naturalized, at the beginning of the War between the States he was given the title of Brigadier General. He boasted of the fact that he was so robust because he never smoked nor drank. He did not need glasses and sometimes surprised comrades by proving to them that he could read by starlight. However, he was sixty-eight. So he presided over the reorganization of his Artillery Battalion and with a tightening of the heart saw it leave without him. Two of his own children and Frederic's five sons were in the Confederate Army. A few months after the regiments' departure, the *Abeille* published a letter from a young Orleanian stating that his camp in Tennessee had been named "Camp Buisson, in honor of our first Captain."

The old soldier was frustrated. Could he not make his adopted country benefit by the teaching he had received at Polytechnique? How could he impart his knowledge to the officers leaving now and to their replacements soon to be needed? Naturally, within half a century conditions had changed. Ammunitions were different. But there were basic principles which a new generation could learn with advantage.

Late at night in his Faubourg Plaisance home, Benjamin Buisson bent over books and notes. One of his daughters might enter his room and ask: "What are you working on so late? Another Napoleon Avenue, or are you studying the stars?" There was no time to waste on streets and stars; the ex-Montereau lieutenant was writing for the soldiers of 1861 his *Instruction pour le Service*

Their Last War

et Manoeuvre de l'Infanterie Légère (Instruction for the Service and Maneuver of Light Infantry).

During the day there was other work to do. News was not good. The fighting was coming closer. The French engineer formed crews from the remaining men and employed them to build a stockade to obstruct passage between the Mississippi and Pontchartrain Lake. To send supplies to this Camp Parapet, as it was called, he had a tunnel dug—as much as it could be dug into that slippery soil—and had it buttressed by thick brick walls. In this climate it would not take long for vines and weeds to grow, and for nature to hastily camouflage the palisade. An enemy coming from the north would have to approach closely to discover the short air-vent atop the powder magazine.

Feverishly Buisson wrote in the same little black book he once used to make notes about crevices cutting through the levee. He had protected the city in peace. He would now protect it in war. On a sketch he wrote: "Three hundred men needed for this garrison, two hundred and twenty-five at the top, twenty-five in reserve, four cannons at this salient." Camp Parapet was ready. The Yankees could come. But would they come this way? During the winter of 1861 a boat going up the river brought a disturbing piece of information. Fishermen sailing through the delta's myriad islets had discovered a group of Union soldiers occupying one of them. A rumor spread that a whole fleet was advancing from the Gulf.

New Orleans was empty of fighting men. Those who had not volunteered at the beginning later answered General Beauregard's appeal. The city had as its only protection 300 men with only three months of training and old muskets. According to official reports, two-thirds of them were French. As in 1814, the question of the foreigners' role in the defense had been raised. Pierre Soulé, whose authority in legal matters was fully recognized, expressed his opinion in a letter to the French Consul, Count de Méjean. It was printed in the *Abeille*. Noncitizens could not be drafted but were at liberty to form their own militia. Méjean wrote to the mayor approving Soulé's views. As in 1815, a French Legion was hastily formed. Someday it would deserve the Orleanians' gratitude. The officers selected as their commander-in-chief Brigadier General Benjamin Buisson. "Excellent choice," the *Daily Picayune* commented.

It was not toward Camp Parapet that the Legion marched. Having been located on the upper side of the river, the fortification could not render the service expected from it since the Federals were coming from the south. The lower part of the Mississippi was in danger. The hope there rested on two forts—one on each bank, Fort Jackson and Fort Philip. From one to the other a barricade made up of tree trunks chained together had been extended. The spring flood with the highest water in years soon destroyed it, and did the same to the barrier boats tied together. The swift currents and eddies coming down the Mississippi seemed to conspire with Admiral Farragut's fleet slowly and meticulously working its way up the river armed with 200 big cannons.

The outside defense once crossed, the interior barricade still stood under Buisson's command. His fourteen cannons looked like toys facing Farragut's advancing thirteen vessels. Buisson gave the order to fire. Grey water harmlessly splashed the ships' hulls. "Fire...fire..." The old officer rushed from one gunner to the other, sensing the futility of his efforts but unwilling to give up his task, as stubborn as on the Montereau battlefield. "Fire!" A hopeless voice answered: "No more ammunition." The burning *La Louisiane* was drifting along exploding like fireworks.

Perhaps the Legionnaires could still render service to the city. Buisson gave an order. They climbed down to the road at the foot of the levee and marched toward New Orleans. The sky was red. The inhabitants had kept their promise. They had set fire to cotton bales, to cases of tobacco, to all products piled on the wharves, rather than to see them fall into the enemy's hands. The French officer must have thought of his friends' description of Moscow in flames. Would New Orleans also destroy itself to repel the invaders? What about his home, his daughters and Albert, his son too young to have gone to war? Breathlessly, he hastened toward the city.

The next day he received a call to report to the French Consulate. Count de Méjean requested a list of all French residents so that he could offer help to the needy. There Benjamin Buisson met Alexis Fecel who had come with his wife and daughter. He asked about some of their former comrades. What about Pierre Charlet? Pierre was still alive, but when one mentioned Captain Charlet now one referred to his son who piloted a fleet of small steamboats on the bayous. Jean Julien Rousseau, a rich merchant, had died aboard ship returning from France. Aware of his desire to be buried in Louisiana ground, his companions had begged the captain not to throw his body into the sea. The deceased had been put into a cask of brandy, and the St. Martinville residents, looking at the wide and short tomb, wondered whether he was still in the improvised coffin. Victor Cherbonnier also had died. The former grenadier of the Guard had asked his family to have him buried standing up, facing the east, in a last salute to his Emperor. Fecel kept talking about friends and places he still visited as the itinerant peddler he had never ceased to be, although doctors had told him, many decades ago, that he had only a few months to live.

Women gathered in the French Consul's antichamber, fearing they might need protection against the victorious General Butler's horrible threats. Fecel and Buisson, silent now, watched the excited group. Had not fate been kind to Cherbonnier, Rousseau and so many other ex-soldiers who had been spared the sight of a new debacle? In the countryside how were other veterans reacting?

In Avoyelles Parish young men entered the school yard. After a quick glance at the classrooms, they went to Adolphe Lafargue's apartment. Loud voices and nervous laughs were heard. They were promising their old master they would show those *"sacrés* Yankees" what a Napoleonic officer's pupils could do. "Good luck, my children!" Lafargue told them, choking with emotion. Those boys were as young as he had been when he had left Orthez to join a hastily formed regiment, the Marie-Louises, adolescents in man-size uniforms over frail bodies. What would happen to those Marie-Louises in grey coats? His Marksville school, modeled after a French lycée—how dull it would be with its upper grades empty. Of course Lafargue's own sons were leaving also. He could not foresee then that they would return unharmed, would continue his work and that, through several generations, the name of Lafargue would remain synonymous with educational progress in that part of Louisiana.

War disturbed even the secluded green nook where Pierre Gabriel Wartelle, a lover of nature and books, still lived. Having become a rich planter of the Washington section of Louisiana, he had sent his sons, one after the other, first to the University of Virginia, then to the Latin Quarter in Paris. Stubbornly, the youngest one had refused to go to France, just as he refused to speak French. This attitude irritated his father until someone remarked: "After all, your youngest one is the most individualistic and therefore the most French of your offspring."

Now all of them were gone. Were they right to take part in the conflict? In the silent house Wartelle would take from a long shelf one of his favorite authors, Montesquieu. *L'Esprit des Lois* (Spirit of the Laws) opened at a frequently read page. "It (slavery) is not good by nature; it is useful neither to the master nor to the slave; to the latter because he does not see the virtue of work, to the former because he acquires among his slaves all kinds of bad habits . . . he becomes vain, reckless, hard, quick-tempered, sensual, cruel." Pierre Gabriel could not recognize himself in this description of a hateful master. Still, he was uneasy when thinking of women and children in the burning sun picking cotton for endless hours. Between the rows of dark faces and little white balls a song would go up, always a lament, a distressing call for help.

Standing in the hall, the door wide open to the soft night, Wartelle heard steps on the avenue where forty years ago he had planted acorns. The moonlight filtered between branches and he saw unfamiliar uniforms. The voices wafted on the night air were harsh. He gave a desperate look at the box which contained his French diplomas, his gold epaulette, his St. Helena medal, pictures, all his treasures. But, after all, were they enemies, those exhausted men looking for shelter? *"Entrez, Messieurs,"* the old gentleman courteously greeted the Union soldiers. Not one of his precious souvenirs nor his beloved books was ever touched by the Yankees. Much later, he received notice that one of his sons had been killed at Shiloh and he envied his colleague, Dr. St. Martin, who had preceded in death his son, Victor, a captain who had fallen at Gettysburg.

Dr. Doussan experienced great anguish also. The war had been over for months and his youngest son had not returned. The family refused to give up hope. One night, when his daughters were entertaining their beaux on the veranda, he saw two shadows moving behind the big magnolia tree. Were they carpetbaggers—or worse? He rushed forward. One of the two men in dirty, tattered clothes, hesitating to appear in full light, was his son, the other was a friend. The Frenchman opened his arms and called in his most vibrant voice: "Don't be ashamed. We were worse off at the Beresina River!"

A short time afterward, this ex-surgeon of the Imperial armies, still suffering from a wound received at Dresden, his health having been affected by wartime deprivations, wrote to Napoleon III asking to be granted the income from a tobacco shop (government property) in some small town where he would end his days. Fecel also, with a hand made clumsy for life by a sword's cut a long time ago, addressed an appeal to the Tuileries Palace. For him and for Dr. Doussan it was now the country of their birth that seemed a peaceful haven. What a disappointment was awaiting them.

The year 1870 brought a shock to all Francophiles. The war against Prussia had been a disaster. The armies had been defeated; Paris was besieged. It was the chastisement Victor Hugo had predicted to anyone who dared to emulate the great Napoleon. Although his nephew had never been liked in Louisiana, the press refrained from throwing stones at the fallen monarch.

Benjamin Buisson must have envisioned Paris once

more occupied by foreign armies. He had never returned there, each additional child making such a possibility more remote. But Cloître St. Méry Street and St. Genevieve Mount were still close to his heart. He was fond of reading about the changes in the French capital. As an architect, he was interested in the wide boulevards Haussmann had opened and in the Opera, of which the new French Opera House in New Orleans was a replica on a small scale.

The double defeat of his two countries, France and Louisiana, had been a hard blow. The Faubourg Plaisance home also had been made sorrowful by a daughter's death. Five children would share the inheritance, but what would it be? Not too much, considering the many years spent in building, printing, writing, surveying, acquiring land and fighting in courts of justice. But what examples of endless energy he and brother Frederic left to their many descendants, all of them sturdy, highly respected citizens.

"Will there be a Waterloo Street, Grandpapa?" a young voice would ask, knowing that the old joke did not bring an outburst of anger any more, but rather a twinkle in the pale blue grey eyes which had become so sad.

"Why not? After all, lost battles have inspired poets more than victories."

In the spring of 1874 Brigadier General Benjamin Buisson died. There was a short obituary in every newspaper, but neither poem nor song. Guillaume Montmain, Tullius de St. Céran and Prosper Foy were no more, and the new generation painfully extricating itself from the Civil War's disasters had neither the time nor the inclination to rhyme and sing. Young Orleanians hardly noticed that the last of the exiles who had fought under Napoleon's golden eagles was now resting in Louisiana soil.

XIII

The Elusive Séraphine

THE SIGHT-SEEING CAR STOPS and the guide announces: "Here we are in front of Napoleon's House, so called because it was going to receive the Emperor. The frigate *La Séraphine* was ready . . ." It was after the death of the last Bonapartist exile that *La Séraphine* set sail, for the first time, through the pages of *Coleman's Guide Book* in 1884. That was about the time Lafcadio Hearn, who resided in New Orleans prior to his departure for Japan, and the novelist George Washington Cable were trying to extract all possible glamor from the French Quarter or Vieux Carré.

The Creoles for whom Cable later became persona non grata were delighted to see attention focused on their city. Defeated during the War Between the States and struggling to hold their own before more and more incoming "foreigners," they found comfort in memories of the past. To think that New Orleans may have been chosen as Napoleon's last refuge, even if it had been a dream, enhanced the city's prestige.

Was *La Séraphine* anything but a dream? No document has been unearthed proving its existence. Naturally, when the St. Helena prisoner was still alive, one could not jeopardize the outcome of the plot and the conspirators' safety by disclosing details. But after 1821, why would one not have revealed the vain attempt?

Three captains have been suggested as having been the expedition's leaders. One was supposed to have been Dominique You. But his close friend, Simon Laignel, in delivering You's funeral oration, did not mention that feat which, even having been a failure, would have added to the buccaneer's glory. If the chief had been a Lieutenant Bossier, known for his bold attacks on the Mexican coast, why did he remain so timidly in the background? If, according to the third version, Jean Laffite himself was to head the rescue party, why would he, so fond of drama and publicity, not have boasted of his role in an undertaking which could have changed the course of history? In addition, no vessel named *La Séraphine* ever appeared in the newspapers of that time.

Yet, people used to speak about "Napoleon's House." There was even a time when a rival home made the same claim. In this contest Nicholas Girod emerged the victor. We may wonder whether, unwittingly, Girod had not benefited from Girard's fame. Girard was a millionaire Bonapartist, a land and ship owner in the delta, although he resided in Philadelphia. On soft Southern tongues the two names sound almost alike.

"Look at that clock," a member of an old Creole family told me, some years ago. "It was placed in what would have been Napoleon's bedroom. That is why my grandfather bought it when the contents of the house at St. Louis and Chartres Streets were sold." The massive, overly ornate clock with all its trimmings was typical of the French Restoration. What proof was there of the illustrious fate it had missed? None, yet the purchaser had a reputation as an intelligent architect, which indicates that the existence of the abortive scheme had been accepted even by enlightened persons.

Both the vessel and the house may be considered as the logical outcome of the legend which, from a human being, created a superman. A superman is able to escape all perils. He is defeated only temporarily; like the Phoenix he can be reborn from his ashes. But to remain a captive seems impossible. This may explain why the stories of *La Séraphine* and the prepared shelter have endured. As dramatic as they were, they still could not completely satisfy popular imagination. Another version sprang up: the buccaneers, indeed, had brought the Emperor to Louisiana.

A few miles from the harbor, across the Mississippi River at the junction of Bayou Laffite and Bayou des Oies, a small mound stands reflected in the calm water. Three tombs were there, and in the 1950s an old woman who spoke French had appointed herself custodian of the little cemetery. She enjoyed talking to strangers, and if one's car stopped nearby there was always a white or black urchin willing to guide one to Madame Perrin's home.

"My great grandfather was one of Laffite's men," she would say, and then add in a whisper: "My daughter does not want me to talk about it, but *I* am proud of it. Don't you think I am right to be proud?"

After being assured that there was nothing more enviable than to have a buccaneer in one's family tree, she would continue: "*Eh bien,* my great grandpapa and thirty-nine sailors"—(why that figure: from forty, as in Oriental tales?)—"left for an island called St. Helena. They traveled for months and months. When they returned, they brought with them a very sick stranger. One day he fell on deck, spitting blood. He died. The coast

The Elusive Séraphine

was not far. The captain himself guided his boat toward this bayou. They stopped near this little hill. All the crew came on shore and with great marks of respect buried the stranger."

"Who was he?"

Here, there was a pause for effect, then the narrator slowly spoke three English words: "The big boss." On the whitewashed walls of Mrs. Perrin's humble room hung a single picture, one of those crude prints in a thick black frame once seen in French farms or village cafés. The old lady pointed to Napoleon's image and with awe said: "The big boss."

We went back to the small cemetery. On the oldest tomb was an iron cross that seemed part of an anchor. "*He* was buried there." Other anecdotes followed. A few years ago, an unknown woman arrived, placed a bunch of violets on the nameless slab and left with Mrs. Perrin a little sum of money for the upkeep of that tomb. Had the legend spread beyond Louisiana?

"Who are the other occupants of this burial place?" the old woman was asked. The answer leaves the questioner amazed. *They* were none other than "his cousins, Jean Laffite and John Paul Jones." To wade through the maze of explanations requires the aid of an article published in August, 1928 by the *New Orleans States*.

Facts or fancies were related by a well-known physician, Dr. Louis Genella, who had the distinction of having been the first American soldier wounded in France in 1917. In his youth, while gliding in a pirogue on the bayous hunting wild ducks, at several isolated stopping places he heard the story of Napoleon's kidnapping. Later on, he traveled through Italy, France and England looking for proof. He found some and, according to his statement, they could have been confirmed through documents hidden in an attic had not the owner, being quite different from Madame Perrin, refused to reveal to the public that she had a pirate among her ancestors.

How could Napoleon, Laffite and John Paul Jones have been related? The rationale behind that enigma could have inspired the most melodramatic play or the weirdest opera libretto. An infant of royal blood had been secretly raised in a Florence monastery at the end of the 18th century and baptized Carlo Buonaparte. He became the father of Charles Bonaparte, whose son was Napoleon. He also had a daughter, Jeanne Corsica, who after many adventures arrived in Louisiana. She married William Paul from Scotland, who was John Paul Jones' brother. Their son took the name Jean Laffite.

In 1819, or so it was alleged, there was indeed a *Séraphine*, but it was only a blind to distract attention from *La Comète* which, commanded by Jean Laffite, reached St. Helena. The vessel was anchored a few miles away. A Malay slave was made a go-between for the Imperial captive and the *Comète*'s captain. Napoleon was urged to wear his wide hat and a long redingote and walk at sunset on a rocky cliff. One evening he saw a shadow climbing toward him. In a rapid sleight of hand, hat and coat were passed from one person to another, and the prisoner slid down the slope into the arms of his relative, Jean Laffite. After many extraordinary incidents, Napoleon died on deck in view of a coast. There Dr. Genella's and Mrs. Perrin's stories meet. It is not likely that the old lady who hardly spoke English would have been able to read the *New Orleans States* articles on that subject. She also must have repeated stories that her parents or grandparents heard from delta fishermen and trappers. Therefore, one can say that *La Séraphine*'s expedition has become part of the lower Mississippi River folklore.

Other Napoleonic mysteries have touched Louisiana.

The Elusive Séraphine

Toward the latter part of the 19th century, an interest in phrenology prompted an examination of Napoleon's death mask. When Antommarchi brought it to New Orleans, no one doubted that he had taken the imprint. But the English physician Francis Burton charged that Marshal Bertrand's wife had packed in her luggage the mask that he, Burton, had made. The controversy did not reach the Louisianians; they were satisfied with Antommarchi's gift. During the Civil War the precious object was hidden, then misplaced. One day a passerby recognized it among junk that had been carted away. He bought it and through families' legacies it was sent to Georgia. About that time a replica, Louis Gally's dearest possession, was located somewhere being used as a doorstop. Finally, through the generosity of the Georgia owner, Antommarchi's mask was retrieved and placed again in the Cabildo where it remains today. It is the actual imprint of the Emperor's face? The question has been raised several times. Whatever the answer, it has its value as the symbol of the strong link between New Orleans and the Napoleonic history and legend.

Another enigma has touched the Deep South. Did Marshal Ney escape to America? The problem belongs to North Carolina where a mysterious Peter Ney, whose handwriting strangely resembled that of Michel Ney, Duke de la Moskowa, suddenly appeared in a village where he became a schoolmaster. Colonel J. J. Lemanowsky recognized him, so he said, but kept the secret well since there was no protest when Lussan published in his *Impériales* a poem to the memory of Ney, a victim of Louis XVIII's firing squad. As a postscript to Ney's mystery, one may add this: about twenty years ago, in a Louisiana community, there was a man who collected everything ever written about the *Grand Maréchal*. He remembered that his great grandmother, Clarice, was the daughter of a Frenchman by the name of Benedict Ney who reached Opelousas before 1820. He married Josephine Belestre (or de Belestre), and shortly after a daughter's birth he disappeared. Clarice always kept in memory of her father a little metal trinket resembling a tiny crown he had placed on her cradle before he left. The souvenir was handed down through generations and one day someone identified it as being the upper part of the Cross on the Legion of Honor.

And, finally, who were the men who named a North Louisiana community Mansura in memory of the Egyptian campaign?

Here and there, names that were famous during the Napoleonic era crop up. In one village the Junots claim relationship with the Duke d'Abrantes. Somewhere a man is proud to be called Marceau like the general who distinguished himself gloriously, but was killed at the time Bonaparte was beginning his ascent to power.

Not many years ago, two elderly ladies died who had been baptized Jena Austerlitz and Lodi Wagram because their Desaix parents (later anglicized to De Seay) proudly stated that they were connected with the heroic young general, instrument and victim of the Marengo victory.

On what battlefields did that flamboyant General Robin gather his stars before he took refuge in Leonville and called one of his sons Napoleon? His portrait in full regalia is still a cherished possession of his descendants, the Chauvins of St. Landry Parish.

One would like to know more about him and about other veterans whose names continue to claim attention. It is a fascinating but endless hunt. Sometimes a clue may lead to a document bearing the Imperial Eagle seal, undeniable proof of its origin; other times the source may be as elusive as the *Séraphine*, one of the fleet of ghostlike ships that will always haunt popular imagination.

Bibliography

I. Primary Sources

THE LARGEST PORTION of primary source material was furnished from documents in the possession of families (unless otherwise stated) and referring to the following: Frederic Buisson; Pierre Benjamin Buisson; Pierre Charlet; Victor Cherbonnier; Dr. Honoré Doussan; Alexis Jules Fecel; L. de Fériet (his letters to his sister Jessica are at the Jefferson County Historical Society, Watertown, N.Y. A typewritten translation is in the Howard-Tilton Library, Tulane University); Henry Ferry; Caius Gracchus Fleuriau's diary (in the possession of Mrs. Chester A. Mehurin); Prosper Foy (Howard-Tilton Library); Marcellin Garand; Louis Gally; Garigues de Flaugeac; Fleury Generelly; Charles François Genin; Albert Jumel (Washington, D.C., National Archives, War Records Division); Joseph Lakanal (Howard-Tilton Library); François Lambert; Dr. Charles Monnot; Dr. Joseph St. Martin; Samuel James Stephens (Covington, Louisiana, St. Tammany Parish Court Records); and Pierre Gabriel Wartelle.

Portraits, medals, mementoes, and other relics about the following were also seen: Benoit Bayard; Louis Gustave Bezou; André Burthe d'Annelet de Rosenthal; Dominique Burthe d'Annelet de Rosenthal; Dominique de Castelnau; Jean David; Dr. Felix Formento; Jean Julien Rousseau; and Louis Surgi.

II. PUBLIC DOCUMENTS

New Orleans, Louisiana. Louisiana State Archives; City Archives; Notarial Archives; St. Louis Cathedral Archives; Registers of the St. Louis Cemeteries; Jackson Barracks Archives; French Consulate General Archives; Tulane University Collection of Favrot Papers, Vol. 12; Cabildo, The Louisiana State Museum; Tomb inscriptions.

Baton Rouge, Louisiana. Louisiana State University Archives.

Covington, Louisiana. St. Tammany Parish Court Records.

New Iberia, Louisiana. Notarial Archives.

Opelousas, Louisiana. Documents of St. Landry Parish; Notarial Archives.

III. NEWSPAPERS

Rare, incomplete series of newspapers published in New Orleans: *Abeille de la Nouvelle Orléans*; *Ami des Lois*; *Argus*; *Courrier de la Louisiane*; *Gazette de la Louisiane*; *Moniteur de la Louisiane*; *Daily Picayune*.

Newspapers published in the parishes (incomplete): *Bannière des Planteurs*; *Courrier de Nachitoches*; *Gazette des Attakapas*; *Gazette des Opelousas*; *Le Meschacebé*; *Le Republicain de Feliciana*; *Le Vigilant*.

Reviews contemporary of the epoch studied are: *Bibliothèque Historique* (Paris); *De Bow's Review* (New Orleans); *Minerve Française* (Paris); *Nemesis Louisianaise* (New Orleans); *Passe Tems* (New Orleans); *Revue des Lyonnais* (Lyon, France); *Revue Louisianaise* (New Orleans).

IV. BOOKS AND ARTICLES

Abrantes, Duchesse d'. *Mémoires sur la Restauration.* Paris, 1836.

Allison, Charles W. "Ney: Was Peter Stewart Ney the Carolina Schoolmaster." *Marshal Michel Ney, the Great French Soldier?* Charlotte, N.C., 1946.

Andrew, Edward L. *Napoleon and America.* New York, 1909.

Arthur, Stanley C. *Old New Orleans.* New Orleans, 1936.

Balzac, Honoré de. *Les Célibataires.* Paris, 1845.

Belisle, A. *Histoire de la Presse Franco-Américaine.* Worcester, Mass., 1911.

Blanchard, Olivia. "Napoleon's Death Mask." *Louisiana Historical Quarterly.* Vol. 9 (1925).

Buisson, Benjamin. *Des Forces qui régissent le système solaire.* New Orleans, 1849.

Burns, Francis. "Lafayette Visits New Orleans." *Louisiana Historical Quarterly.* Vol. 29 (1946).

Carmer, Carl. *Stars Fell on Alabama.* New York, 1934.

Castellanos, H. C. *New Orleans as It Was.* New Orleans, 1895.

Caulfield, Ruby Van Allen. *The French Literature in Louisiana.* New York, 1929.

Cherbonnier, Pierre. *Alphabet.* New Orleans, 1829.

Childs, Frances Sergeant. *French Refugees' Life in the United States.* Baltimore, 1940.

Claiborne, W. C. C. *Official Letter Book, 1775–1817.* Edited by Dunbar Rowland. Jackson, Miss., 1917.

Clapp, Theodore. *Autobiographical Sketches and Recollections During a Thirty Years' Residence in New Orleans.* Boston, 1857.

Clark, T. Wood. *Émigrés in the Wilderness.* New York, 1941.

Coleman, Will H. *Historical Sketch Book and Guide of New Orleans and Environs.* New York, 1884.
Confederate Military History Written by Distinguished Men of the South. Edited by Clement Evans. Atlanta, Ga., 1899.
Connelly, Owen. *The Gentle Bonaparte.* New York, 1968.
Couper, Col. William. *Claudius Crozet, Soldier, Scholar, Educator, Engineer, 1789–1864.* Charlottesville, Va., 1936.
David, Urbain de Cette. *Les Anglais à la Louisiane en 1814–1815.* New Orleans, 1845.
Dawson, John Charles. *Lakanal the Regicide.* Tuscaloosa, Ala., 1948.
———. "The Vine and Olive Colony." *French Review.* Vol. 28 (December, 1944).
Dechamp, Jules. *La Légende Napoléonienne.* Paris, 1931.
Dennery, General. "Conférence de Musée de l'Armée." *Bulletin de la Société de Amis du Musée de L'Armée.* No. 8 (July 1913).
Duboully, P. L. Aubry. *Le-Champ d'Asile ou les Militaires Français refugies en Texas.* Words by J. J. C. Music by Aubry Duboully, Paris. No date.
Durel, L. C. "Les Journalistes des Paroisses Louisianaises." *Le Bayou.* No. 30, Houston, Tex.
Ebeyer, P. B. *Escape from St. Helena.* New Orleans, 1947.
Fortier, Alcee. *A History of Louisiana.* New York, 1904.
Frost, Meigs O. "Says Laffite Snatched Corsican from Isle." *New Orleans States.* 19 August 1928.
———. "How Laffite Whisked Napoleon from Isle." *New Orleans States.* 28 August 1928.
Gayarré, Charles. *Fernando de Lemos.* New York, 1872.
Girard, Just. *The Adventures of a French Captain, At Present a Planter in Texas.* Paris, 1858. Translated by Lady Blanche Murphy. New York, 1878.

Gorce, Henry de la. *Louis XVIII*. Paris, 1926.
Guillot, Dr. Lucien. *Le Général Lefebvre-Desnouettes*. Alencon, France, 1961.
Hanna, A. J. *A Prince in Their Midst*. Oklahoma University Press, 1947.
Hartmann, _____, and Miller, _____. *Le Texas ou notice sur le Champ d'Asile*. Paris, 1819.
Héritier, L. F. *Le Champ d'Asile*. Paris, 1819.
Hudry, Jean-Claude. *Un émigrant Chablaisien, 1774–1832*. Annecy, France, 1886. Extracts from Hudry's diary published by Fr. Mignet.
Hyde de Neuville, Jean Guillaumé. *Mémoires et Souvenirs de Baron Hyde de Neuville*. Paris, 1893–1912.
Jouin, H. *Lakanal en Amérique d'après sa correspondance inédite, 1815–1837*. Besançon, France, 1904.
Kendall, John Smith. *History of New Orleans*. Chicago and New York, 1922.
———. "Piracy in the Gulf of Mexico, 1816–1823." *Louisiana Historical Quarterly*. Vol. 8 (1925).
King, Grace. *New Orleans, the Place and the People*. New York, 1895.
Lafargue, Andre. "Napoléon est-il aux Invalides?" *Comptes-rendus de l'Athénée Louisianais*. (January–May, 1932).
Laignel, Simon. *The Extempore Funeral Oration Pronounced at the Grave of the Famous Captain Dominique You, by His Old Friend, Simon Laignel*. New Orleans, 1830.
Lallemand, General Charles. "Lettre de Champ d'Asile." *Bibliothèque Historique*. Vol. 4 (11 May 1818).
———. "Napoléon refuse de passer en Amérique." *French-American Review*. Vol. 11 (April–June, 1949). Extracts from the journal of General Charles

Frederic Antoine Lallemand, July–August 1816.
Lanusse, A. *Les Cenelles.* New Orleans, 1845.
Latour, Major A. Lacarrière. *Historical Memoirs of the War in West Florida and Louisiana in 1814–1815.* Translated by H. P. Nugent, Philadelphia, 1816.
Latrobe, B. H. *The Journal of B. H. Latrobe, 1796–1820.* New York, 1905.
Laussat, Pierre Clement de. *Mémoires sur ma vie à mon fils pendant les années de 1813 et suivantes.* Pau, France, 1831.
Lepouzé, Constant. *Poésies Diverses.* New Orleans, 1838.
Lote, G. "La Mort de Napoléon et l'opinion publique en 1821." *Revue des Etudes Napoléoniennes.* (June 1930).
Louisiana Book. *The Selections from the Literature of the States.* Edited by Th. McCaleb. New Orleans, 1894.
Louisiana State Museum Publication. *Death Mask of Napoleon.* (15 January 1936).
Lussan, Auguste. *Les Impériales.* New Orleans, 1841.
McCortney, C. R., and Dorance, Gordon. *The Bonapartes in America.* Philadelphia, 1939.
McMaster, J. B. The Life and Times of Stephen Girard. Philadelphia, 1918.
Martin, François Xavier. *The History of Louisiana.* New Orleans, 1882.
Martin, P. "Le Champ d'Asile." *Revue des Lyonnais.* Vol. V (September 1838).
Martin, Thomas W. *French Military Adventurers in Alabama, 1818–1828.* Birmingham, Ala., 1937.
Montlezun, Baron de. *Voyage fait dans les années 1816–1817 de New York à la Nouvelle Orléans.* Paris, 1818.
Montulé, Edouard de. *Voyage to North America and the West Indies in 1817.* Translated. London, 1821.

Noble, Stuart G. "School of New Orleans During the First Quarter of the Nineteenth Century." *Louisiana Historical Quarterly.* Vol. 14 (1931).

Official Records of the Union and Confederate Armies in the War of the Rebellion, 1861–1865. N. p., n. d.

Overdyke, W. Darnell. "History of the American Party in Louisiana." *Louisiana Historical Quarterly.* Vol. 15 (1932).

Pardée, M. A. *L'Etrange histoire du masque de Napoléon le Grand.* Cannes, 1932.

Philips, Edith. *Les Refugiés Bonapartistes en Amérique, 1815–1830.* Paris, 1923.

Picket, Albert James. *History of Alabama.* Charleston, S.C., 1851.

Reeves, Jesse S. *The Napoleonic Exiles in America.* Baltimore, 1905.

Revised Code of Louisiana with Amendments. Edited by E. E. Saunders. New Orleans, 1920.

Rosengarten, J. G. *French Colonists and Exiles in the United States.* Philadelphia, 1907.

St. Céran, Tullius de. *Chansons et poesies diverses.* New Orleans, 1836.

———. *Rien ou Toi.* New Orleans, 1837.

———. *1814–1815 ou les Combats de la Victoire des Fils de Louisiane.* New Orleans, 1838.

Sang Royal de France (extraits de documents du Ministere de la Guerre à Paris concernant André Burthe d'Annelet de Rosenthal et sa famille.) N. p., n. d.

Saucier, C. L. *History of Avoyelles Parish, Louisiana.* New Orleans, 1943.

Sennegy, René de. *St. Michel du comte d'Acadie.* New Orleans, 1877.

Story of Champ d'Asile as Told by Two of the Colonists.

Translated and edited by F. E. Ratchford. Book Club of Texas, 1937.

Testut, Charles. *Les Echos.* New Orleans, 1849.

———. *Fleurs d'Eté.* New Orleans, 1851.

Tinker, Edward Laroque. *Les Écrits de Langue Française en Louisiane au XIXe siécle.* Paris, 1932.

———. *Bibliography of French Newspapers in Louisiana.* Worchester, Mass., 1933.

Valaun, C. "La Légende Napoléonienne aux Etats-Unis." *Mercure de Fr.* (15 January, 1925).

Vasson, Jacques de. *Bertrand, le grand maréchal de Ste-Helene.* Issoudun, France, 1935.

Waitz, Julia Ellen. *The Journal of Julia Legrand, 1862–1863.* Edited by Kate Mason Rowland and Mrs. Morris L. Crowall. Richmond, 1911.

Whitfield, G. Jr. *"The French Grant in Alabama: A History of the Founding of Demopolis."* Alabama Historical Society, 1899–1903.

Wildes, Harry Emerson. *Lonely Midas: The Story of Stephen Girard.* New York, 1943.

Yakum, ———. *A Comprehensive History of Texas.* Vol. 1, 1695–1845. Original text notes and new notes and introduction by Seth Shepard. Washington, 1896.

Index

Since Napoleon I, under various titles, is mentioned frequently in the text, specific references are omitted in the index. The name New Orleans also is omitted since it is the locale of most of the chapters.

Abeille Américaine (or American Bee) (newspaper), 128
Abeille de la Nouvelle Orléans (Bee) (newspaper), 128, 143, 146–148, 159, 163, 174–175, 177, 184
Advertiser, The (newspaper), 156
Aigleville, 63
Aime, Valcour, 118
Alabama (ship), 171
Albino (ship), 96
Alexander, Czar, 167
Alexandria, La., 160
Alphabet (Pierre Cherbonnier), 130–131, 159
Ambrogia (café), 151
Amenity Lodge, 128
American Theater, 163
Amérique (ship), 4, 15
Ami des Lois (newspaper), 32, 37, 60, 72, 74, 130
Amis de Béranger (club), 166
Amis des Noirs (club), 181
Anecdotes (de Beausset), 126
Antommarchi, Dr. Francesco (or Francisco), 87, 89, 93, 121, 126, 145–149, 197
Antonio de Sedilla, Fra, see Père Antoine
Arceneaux family, 111
Atala (Châteaubriand), 14
Attakapas, 112, 166
Attakapas (ship), 135
Audubon, Jean Jacques, 93
Aurora (newspaper), 87

Austerlitz (domain), 118
Avoyelles Parish, 124, 188

Baillon, de, 114–115
Barataria Bay (and the Baratarians), 27, 70, 72
Barnett, Maurice, 40, 164, 168, 184
Battle, The (Battle of New Orleans), vii, 27, 85, 97, 133, 183
Bayard, Benoit Baron, and sons Alfred and Hyppolite, 112
Bayou Boeuf, 172
Bayou Cocodrie, 127
Bayou Courtableau, 116, 172
Bayou des Oies, 194
Bayou Laffite, 194
Bayou Lafourche, 108–109
Beauharnais, Hortense de; Queen of Holland, 177
Beauharnais, Josephine de, see Bonaparte, Josephine
Beauregard, Général Pierre Toutans de, 185
Beausset, de, 126
Bédoyère, Charles de la (or de Labédoyère), 37
Bee (newspaper), see Abeille
Belestre, Josephine de, 198
Belle Alliance, xv, 109
Belle Poule (ship), 159, 161
Béranger, Pierre Jean de, 13, 125, 129, 165–167
Bernadotte, Jean; King of Sweden, 152

Bernard, Général Simon, 51–52, 142
Bernard, Stephen, 165
Bernardin de St. Pierre, 13
Bertrand, Arthur, 167
Bertrand, Madame, 167, 197
Bertrand, Marshal Henri, 145, 147, 167
Bertrand, Napoleon, 167
Bezou, Louis Gustave, 109
Bienville, Jean Baptiste de, 17
Blanc, Antoine, 165
Blanc, Archbishop, 161
Blanc d'Erneville, 112
Blenk, Archbishop, 110
Blieux, de, 113
Blücher, General, 11
Boismare, Antoine Louis, 125, 127, 129–130
Bonaparte, Caroline; Madame Murat; Queen of Naples, 64, 150
Bonaparte, Charles, 196
Bonaparte, Joseph; King of Spain; Count de Survilliers, 12–13, 38, 54–56, 78, 80, 87, 102, 105, 151
Bonaparte, Josephine; née Tascher de la Pagerie; widow de Beauharnais; Madame Bonaparte; Empress, 20, 22, 34, 37, 136, 160
Bonaparte, Laetitia; Madame Mère, 149
Bonaparte, Louis; King of Holland, 177
Bonaparte, Louis Napoleon, see Napoleon, 111
Bonaparte, Napoleon, see note at beginning of index
Bonaparte, Pauline; Paulette; Madame Leclerc; Princess
Bon Sens, Le (newspaper), 163
Bordentown, 55
Borghese, 24–25, 91
Bossier, Lieutenant, 193
Bouchelle, Victor de, 164
Boudreaux family, 111
Bourdin, Bernard, 156
Bourgeois, Josephine, 111
Boyé, 77
Broussard family, 111
Brown, Dr., of Kentucky, 53
Buffon, Georges Louis Leclerc de, 103
Buisson, Albert, 187
Buisson, Benjamin (Pierre Benjamin), vi; arriving in New Orleans, 8; previous experiences, 9–17; new contacts, 19–45; architect, 44–47; reorganizing the Orleans Battalion, 48–50, 70, 80; marriage, 81, 85, 87, 89, 91–92, 99, 102, 104, 106, 107; newspaper publisher in Natchitoches, 120–122; printer and publisher in New Orleans, 130–131; surveyor and engineer, 138–140; chief engineer of the State of Louisiana 146–150; commander of the Legion, 155, 157, 161; writing about astronomy, 169–170; brigadier general and writing a military treatise, 184–185; Camp Parapet, 185; Commander of the French Legion, 186, 190; death, 191
Buisson, Elizabeth; Isabella; née Guillotte, 6, 49, 59, 81, 88, 121
Buisson, Frédéric, 8, 49–50, 59; marriage, 81, 121, 138, 155, 181; sons, 184, 191
Buisson, Jean François Claude, 8
Buisson, Marie Esther, née Guillotte, 8, 15, 49
Buisson, Sophie, née Guillotte, 6, 49, 59, 81, 88, 90, 131
Buisson, Sophie (daughter), 124
Buonaparte, Carlo, 196
Buonaparte, Napoleon Frederick, 148
Burthe, André d'Annelet de Rosenthal, 19, 49
Burthe, Dominique d'Annelet de Rosenthal, 50, 141
Burton, Dr. Francis, 145, 197
Butler, General, 188
Buys de, 177

Cabildo, 72, 147, 197
Cable, George Washington, 192
Caillou, Pierre, 34, 36, 45, 61, 79, 86, 159
Calaboose, 72, 74, 97, 156
Camp Buisson, 184
Camp Parapet, 185–186
Canbronne, General Pierre, 152
Cane River, 124
Canonge, Judge Jean Francois, 93, 165
Canonge, Placide, 165
Canova, Antonio, 80
Carnot, Lazare, 9
Caroline, see Bonaparte, Caroline
Caroline, Queen of England, 88
Castelnau, Dominique de, 177

Index

Caveau, Le (café), 40
Cavelier, Zenon, 71
Celluri, Captain, 32
Chalmette (The Battle), 133
Chambray, Marquis de, 126
Champ d'Asile, 13, 57–58, 60–62, 66–67, 69, 71–72, 75–77, 123, 165
Chants du siècle, 127
Chapman, Mrs., 183
Chardon, 39
Charity Lodge, 50, 91, 93
Charles X, 134, 175
Charlet, Captain, 187
Charlet, Pierre, xv, xvi, 109, 111, 127, 187
Charvet, Lucien, 106
Chassepot, Le (ship), 57
Châteaubriand, François René de, 14, 129
Châtiments, Les (V. Hugo), 179
Chaudron, Simon, 128
Chauvin family, 198
Chenet, 69
Cherbonnier, Pierre, 72, 77, 130–131, 159
Cherbonnier, Victor, 41, 123, 176, 187
Cheret, 91–92
Christophe, 24
Claiborne, Governor W. C. C., 21–22, 27, 32
Claiborne, Madame, 27
Clapp, Reverend Theodore, 158
Clary, Desiree, 152
Clausel (or Clauzel), General Bertrand, 29, 52, 54–57, 61, 64–65, 114
Clinton, La., 143
Clouet, de, 112
Code Napoléon, vii, 71, 153
Coleman's Guide Book, 192
Collège de la Louisiane, 131
Collège d'Orléans (Orleans College), 102–104, 122, 135, 141, 157, 164–165
Comète, La (ship), 196
Confédération Napoléonienne, 78
Conner, 163
Corsica, Jeanne, 196
Courcelle, Leon, 177
Courrier de la Louisiane (newspaper), 16, 18, 32, 42, 52, 70, 77, 85–89, 95, 135–136, 156, 161, 166–167
Courrier de la Nouvelle Orléans (newspaper), 171, 174, 179
Courrier de Natchitoches (newspaper), 122, 130, 157

Courrier des Etats Unis (newspaper), 87
Crossiac, 60–61
Crozet, Colonel Claudius, 140–141; as a railroad builder, 143–144, 168
Custom House, 46–47
Cuvelier (or Cuvellier), Colonel Charles, 43, 66, 104, 106, 130, 171
Cuvelier (or Cuvellier), Virginie, 88
Cuvillier, Adolphe, 154

D'Abrantes, Duc, *see* Junot
Daily Advertiser (newspaper), 153
Daily Picayune (newspaper), 186
D'Annelet, Monsieur, *see* Sarpy, Marguerite Suzanne D'Autrichy, 87
David, Jean, 120–121
David, Sarah, 120
David, Urbain de Cette, 164, 178
Davis, John, 5, 91
De Bow's Review, 98
De Buonaparte et des Bourbons (Châteaubriand), 129
Delord Sarpy, *see* Sarpy
Demopolis, 62–64
Deron, Elie, 169
Desaix, General Louis, 153, 198
Descartes, Rene, 169
Desfarges, 73
Des Forces qui regissent le Système Solaire (Buisson), 169
Desforges, Consul, 22
Deshoulières, Madame, 131
Dessalines, 24
Destrehan, Nicolas, 71
Donaldsonville, 90, 176
Dorfeuille, 82, 129
Doussan, Dr. Honoré, 92, 105, 178, 190
Dubourg, Dr., 92
Dufour, Dr., 92
Dugarry, Captain J. F., 176
Dumez, Eugene, 155
Dumez, Jean Baptiste, 155
Dumond, Emilie Constance, 110
Dumouriez, General Charles, 22
Duval, Colonel Leon, 127

Ecoles Centrales (central schools, later called Lycées), 102–103
Ecole des Chartes, 169
Ecole Normale Supérieure, 101
Ecole Polytechnique, 9, 15, 42, 58, 102, 140, 184

Eglise de l'Assomption (Assumption Church), xv
Emerson, Ralph Waldo, 152
Encyclopedists, 9, 117
Eudes de Gentilly, Dr., 75, 105, 149
Evangeline (Longfellow), 111
Exilés, Café des, 21

Fain, Baron, 126
Farragut, Admiral, 186
Faubourg St. Mary, 137
Faubourg Plaisance, 138, 184
Favrot, Philogene, 39
Favrot, Pierre Joseph (Don Pedro), 39
Fecel, Alexis Jules, 118–121, 187–188, 190
Feriet, de, 72, 79, 105
Ferrand, Captain, 121
Ferry, Henry, 166
Fête de François (S. Chaudron), 128
Feuilles d'automne (Hugo), 169
Feuilles d'été (Testut), 169
Fleuriau, Caius Gracchus, 79, 92
Fleury, Cardinal, 83
Florville, 182
Fontainebleau (Marigny estate), 154
Fontainebleau Military School, 117
Fontenot, Louis (Big Louis), 114–116
Fontenot, Marie Louise, *see* Garrigues de Flaugeac, Marie Louise
Formento, Dr. Felix, 75–77, 87, 92, 105, 146, 149
Formento, Dr. (Felix's son), 180
Formento, Madame (Boutte widow), 88
Fort Rouge, *see* Red Fort
Fouchardière, Abbe de la (Rene de Sennegy), 141–143
Foy, General Maximilien, 126
Foy, Prosper, 109, 163, 191
Frelon, Le (newspaper), 128
Frelon (ship), 121
Fuzelier de la Claire, 112

Gaines, General, 170
Gally, Brutus, 41
Gally, Louis, 41, 49, 60, 68, 153–155, 170, 176–177, 181
Galveston, 58, 68, 76, 111
Garden District, 137
Gareau, Armand, 169
Garrigues de Flaugeac, Adolphe, 116; as Judge Garrigues, 173

Garrigues de Flaugeac, Antoine, 29–30, 91, 100, 113–116, 173
Garrigues de Flaugeac, Celeste, 116
Garrigues de Flaugeac, Claire, 116
Garrigues de Flaugeac, Madame, *née* Marie Louise Fontenot, 115, 172
Gazette de Baton Rouge, 166
Gazette de la Louisiane, 16, 18, 32, 59–60, 65, 85–86, 93, 150
Gazette des Opelousas, 165
Genella, Dr. Louis, 195–196
Generelly, Fleury Theotime de Rinaldi, 82–85, 87, 89, 127, 155, 181
Generelly, Madame, 90
Genin, Charles Francois, 116–117
Gentilly, 137
Geoffroy St. Hilaire, 103, 116, 182
George IV, 87
Gerard, General Etienne, 63
Germain, H. (Henri?), 165
Gettysburg, 190
Girard, Just, 69–70
Girard, Stephen, 80, 96, 153, 193
Giraudon, 163
Girod Nicolas, 33, 79, 149, 159, 193
Gleize Langdac, 82, 85
Gourrier, Dr., 110
Gradenico, Marchese, 117
Gradenico, Marguerite, 117
Grand Terre (or Grande Terre), 65, 70, 72, 77, 98, 130
Grenadiers Français, Les (play), 72
Gretry, André, 72
Greuze, Jean Baptiste, 82
Grouchy, Marshal Count Emmanuel de, 63
Grouchy, Victor de, 63
Guerrier Intrépide, Le (V.de Bouchelle), 164
Guillemin, François (Consul), 39, 60–61, 78–80, 88
Guillot, Pierre, 102, 104, 106, 134
Guillotte, Alexandre, 8
Guillotte, Alexandre Pierre ("cousin Guillotte"), 5, 15–17, 23, 25, 39–40, 49–50, 60, 77
Guillotte, Elizabeth (Isabella), *see* Buisson, Elizabeth
Guillotte, Marie Esther, *see* Buisson, Marie Esther
Guillotte, Marie Petronille, 6
Guillotte, Pierre, 6
Guillotte, Sophie, *see* Buisson, Sophie

Index

Harpe, Bernard de la, 131
Harper's Weekly (review), 167
Hartmann, 68
Hausmann, Baron Georges, 191
Hauterive, de, 112
Hearn, Lafcadio, 192
Heritier, 68, 70, 166
Hernani (V. Hugo), 58
Herrera, Manuel, 58
Hoche, General Lazare, 24
Hortense, *see* Beauharnais, Hortense de
Houssaye, de la, 112
Huchet de Kernion, 37
Hudry, Jean Claude, 43, 79
Hugo, Victor, 118, 129, 160, 165–167, 176–178, 183, 190
Hulot, Mademoiselle, 22
Humbert, General Jean Joseph Amable (or Jean Amable), 23–28, 30, 38, 50, 58, 68, 71–74, 91–96, 98, 170
Hyde de Neuville, 39, 78

Impériales, Les, (Lussan), 167, 197
Imperial Prince, 179
Institut de France, 102–103
Instructions pour le service et manoeuvre de l'Infanterie légère (Buisson), 185
Isle d'Orleans, 18, 21

Jackson, General Andrew, vii, 30–31, 153, 163
Jaune, Urbain, 85
Jeannin, Jean Baptiste, 42, 87, 92, 101–102, 104
Jefferson College, 141, 144
Jefferson (suburb), 138
Jesuits, 138, 188
Joinville, Prince de, 161
Jones, John Paul, 195
Jones, William, 195
Joseph, *see* Bonaparte, Joseph
Josephine, *see* Bonaparte, Josephine
Journal du Commerce, 131
Journal historique de l'établissement des Français, 131
Journée des 3 Empereurs (or *Veille d'Austerlitz*) (drama), 38
Jumel, Alfred, 144
Junot, Andoche, Duc d'Abrantes, 188, 198

King of Rome (Roi de Rome); Duke de Reichstadt; Napoleon II, 10, 88, 129, 135–136

Labedoyère, Charles; Colonel then General; Count de (also de la Bedoyère), 37
La Boissière, 144
Lacarrière, Latour de, 29–30
Lacordaire, Henri, 142
Lafargue, Adolphe, 123–124, 188
Lafayette, George Washington de, 106–122, 174–175
Lafayette, Marquis Gilbert de, vii, 106–107
Lafayette, (suburb), 138
Laffite, Jean, 26–27, 30, 58, 68, 70, 72–73, 75–77, 98, 111, 130, 194–196
Laffite, Pierre, 30, 65, 70, 73, 81, 98
Lafitte, Jacques, 65, 80, 96
Lagarde, 72
L'Aiglon (Rostand), 129
Laignel, Simon, 98, 131–132, 193
Lakanal, Joseph, 36, 79, 101–106, 122, 141, 149, 182
Lakanal, Madame, 106
Lake Borgne, 137
Lake Pontchartrain, 52, 137, 139, 144
Lalaurie, Dr., 148
Lallemand, General; Baron Charles, 38, 52, 56–58, 60, 62, 66–68, 70–72, 77–79, 92, 95, 98, 105, 130, 144
Lallemand, Henri, 52, 56–57, 79–80, 96
Lamartine, Alphonse de, 129, 174
Lambert, François, 41
Lambertin (café), 12, 40
Lancaster, 42
Lannes, Marshal Jean, 153
Laplace, Pierre Simon de, 170
Las Cases, Emmanuel; Count de, 86
Latil, Alexandre, 166
Latrobe, Benjamin Henry, 44, 51, 77
Latrobe, Henry, 46, 141
Laurent, 123
Laurent, Madame, 123
Laussat, Pierre Clement de, 19
Lavaud, Charles, 68
Lavoisier, Antoine Laurent de, 9
Leclerc, Marshal Charles, 25, 29, 114, 131, 181
Leclerc, Madame, *see* Bonaparte, Pauline
Lefebvre-Desnouettes, General; Count; Charles, 11, 38, 52, 55–57, 62, 64–65, 91–92, 96, 98

Legion (*see also* Orleans Battalion), 97, 99, 105, 107, 135, 154, 160, 171, 181, 184
Légion des Français (French Legion), 186
Lemanowsky, Colonel J. J., 160, 197
Le Monnier, Dr. Yves, 156–157
Lepouzé, Constant, 164–165
Leverrier, Urbain, 170
Life of Père Antoine, 131
Livaudais, Enoul de, 17, 81
Livaudais, Jacques de, 17, 81
Livingston, Judge, 153
Louis IX, 3
Louis XIV, 112
Louis XV, 83
Louis XVI, 15, 101, 116
Louis XVIII, 12, 31–32, 36–38, 41, 52, 106, 140, 160, 197
Louis-Philippe I (former Duke of Orleans), 52, 65, 96, 134, 145, 159, 175
L'ouverture (or Louverture), Toussaint, 24, 181
Lowe, Sir Hudson, 80, 145
Lussan, Auguste, 167

Madame Mère, *see* Bonaparte, Laetitia
Maid of Orleans (paddle boat), 82
Manon Lescaut (Abbé Prevost), 13
Mansura, 155, 198
Manuel de Géographie élementaire, 131
Marceau, General Francois, 198
Marengo County, 61–62
Marie Antoinette, Queen, 42
Marie Louise, Empress, 20, 89, 136
Marigny, Bernard de, 23, 30, 105, 134, 136–137
Marigny family, 154
Marigny, Mandeville de, 154
Marksville, 124
Martin, Father, 124
Martin, François Xavier, 71
Mayflower (ship), 18
Mazureau, Dominique, 34–35
McDonough (schooner), 54
McKittrick, Anne, 120
Mejean, Count de (Consul), 186–187
Mémoires (Antommarchi), 149
Mémorial (Napoleon), 127
Mercier, 168
Mestier, David, 53

Michoud, Antoine, 137, 168
Milliard, 68
Milneburg, 144, 168
Milne Home for Destitute Boys, 171
Minerve Française, La (ship), 13–14, 53, 55, 57, 67, 70
Mobile, 63–65, 106, 182
Molon, Cadet, 5
Moniteur, Le (newspaper), 19
Monnot, Dr. Joseph, 92, 110–111, 183
Monroe, President, 102
Montagnac, Emilie de, 109
Montereau, 11–12, 184–186
Montesquieu, Charles de la Brede de, 117, 189
Montiasse, 41
Montluzin, Baron de, 38–39
Montmain, Guillaume, 89, 92, 125, 129, 164, 171, 181, 191
Morandière, de la, 113
Moreau, General Jean Victor Marie, 22–23, 29
Moreau-Lislet, L., 71
Moutons, Les (Deshoulières), 131
Murat, Prince Achille, 113, 150–152
Murat, Caroline Bonaparte, Queen of Naples, *see* Bonaparte, Caroline
Murat, General Joachim, King of Naples, 29, 113, 150–152
Musée, Le, 82

Napoleon I, *see* note at beginning of index
Napoleon II, *see* King of Rome
Napoleon III, (Bonaparte, Louis Napoleon), 179–180, 190
Napoléon à Ste Hélène (drama), 163
Napoleon Avenue, 139
Napoleon, (café), 78
Napoleon's house, 192–193
Napoleon le Petit (V. Hugo), 179
Napoleon ou Vive l'Empereur (drama), 163
Napoleonville, 110–111
Natchez (ship), 59, 107, 122
Natchitoches (Nakitosh), 59, 76, 121, 124
National Intelligencer (newspaper), 54
Native American Party (or American Party), 162, 170, 176
Neptune, Le (ship), 121
New Orleans, *see* note at beginning of index

Index

New Orleans States (newspaper), 195–196
Ney, Benedict, 197
Ney, Clarice, 197
Ney, Michel, Duke de la Moscowa, 152, 160, 197
Ney, Peter Stewart, 197
Nicolas, Adolphe, 127
Niles' Weekly Register, 64
Northumberland (ship), 78

Octoroons' Ball, 5, 76
Ode aux Défenseurs de la Nouvelle Orléans (S. Chaudron), 127–128
Old Kettle (Simon Chaudron), 128
Olivier de Vezin, 112
O'Meara, Dr., 87
Onis, Luis de, 78
Opelousas, 91, 100, 112, 114–117, 158, 198
Orcagna, 158
O'Reilly, Governor, 74
Orleans Ballroom, 88
Orleans Battalion, 99, 153–155, 161, 170–172, 176, 184, see also Legion
Orleans College, see Collège d'Orléans
Orleans, Duke of, 17, 134
Orleans Theater, see Théâtre d'Orléans

Parmentier, Nicholas, 53–54
Passe-Tems (newspaper), 125–127, 129
Pauger, 138
Paul et Virginie (Bernardin de St. Pierre), 13
Paul, William, 196
Pauline, La (ship), 32
Pennières, 36, 53, 68, 70, 72
Père Antoine (Fra Antonio de Sedilla), 5, 80–81, 92, 97, 132
Perché, Napoleon Joseph, Archbishop, 110
Perdreauville, de, 42, 181
Perdreauville, Madame, 131
Perrin, Madame, 194–196
Philadelphia, 56, 65, 78, 80, 102, 128
Pichegru, General Charles, 22
Pilié, Joseph, 139
Plattenville, 126
Point Breeze, 56
Pointe Coupee, 118
Porion, 41, 66

Port Hudson, 143
Prevost, Abbé, 13
Prévost, Dr. François, 110
Prieur, Denis (Mayor), 147

Racine, Jean, 117
Raoul, Colonel Nicolas, 61, 64, 120
Ravel, Bruno, 6, 86
Ravesies, Frederic, 63
Red Fort (Fort Rouge), 58, 77, 98
Reichstadt, Duc de, see King of Rome
Renou, Urbain, 77
Rigaud, General Antoine, 57, 66, 77, 92, 95, 98
Rigaud de Vaudreuil, Marquis, xviii
Rigaud, Marie, 66, 95
Rigaud, Narcisse Pericles, 67–68, 71, 95
Roaldes, Dr. Arthur, 172
Robin, General, 198
Roffignac, Count de, 44, 92, 101
Roi de Rome, see King of Rome
Roman, Andre Bienvenu, Governor, 147
Rostand, Edmond, 129
Rouquette, Adrien, 164
Rouquette, Dominique, 164–166
Rousseau, Jean Jacques, 13, 82, 103, 113, 117
Rousseau, Jean Julien, 112, 187
Ruy Blas (V. Hugo), 166

Sabine River, 69–70, 170
St. Ceran, Tullius de, 101, 164–166, 191
St. Charles Hotel, 168
St. Gème, Major, 163
St. Helena medal, xvi, 179–180, 189
St. John the Baptist Parish, 90
St. Landry Parish, 173, 198
St. Louis Cathedral, 3, 45–46, 71, 80–81, 89, 91–92, 162–163
St. Louis Cemetery, 132
St. Louis Hotel, 161
St. Martin (St. Martinville), 112, 187
St. Martin, Dr. Joseph, 90, 92, 110, 190
St. Martin, Victor, 190
St. Maurice, 135
St. Michel (parish), 141
St. Napoleon (church), 110
Salem (ship), 146–147, 149

San Antonio de Campeche (ship), 65, 68
San Domingo, xvi, 20–21, 23, 31, 42, 85, 87, 97, 109, 113, 132, 156, 163, 181
Sarpy, Delord, 50
Sarpy, Marguerite Suzanne Delord, 49
Sarpy, Louise, 50
Schamburg, Lieutenant, 154
Schwartzenberg, General, 11
Scott, Sir Walter, 126
Seghers, Dominique, 35
Segur de, 126
Sennegy, René de, see Fouchardière
Séraphine, La (ship), 192–194, 196, 198
Serurier (or Serrurier), 26, 32
Servant, Alexandre, 151
Shiloh, 190
Sinabaldi, Marchioness de and children, 64
Société agricole et mécanique, 56, 61
Société du Vin et de l'Olive, (Vine and Olive Colony), 61, 128
Soulé, Pierre, 176, 186
State Militia, 172
Stephens, Samuel James, 120
Superbe, La (ship), 80
Surgi, Louis, 155
Survilliers, Count de, see Bonaparte, Joseph

Taillefer, 38
Tascher de la Pagerie, see Bonaparte, Josephine
Tasset, 109
Taylor, General Zachary, 170, 176
Tell, William, 175
Temps, Le (newspaper), 135
Testut, Charles, 166, 169
Théâtre d'Orléans (Orleans Theater), 17, 38, 91, 146, 150, 163, 167
Théâtre St. Philippe, 33
Thiot (also Café), 23
Tiernant, Marquis de, 126
Tilly, de, 113
Tombigbee River, 53, 55–57, 60–61, 63, 65, 108
Tournaire, Jean Baptiste, 148
Tousac (or Touzac), Chevalier Anne Louis de, 26, 31–33, 35–36
Transylvania University, 104
Tremoulet Hotel, 51–52, 55, 57, 61, 65, 71, 77–78, 110, 141
Tremoulet, Madame, 51
Trinity River, 57, 108
Turpin (also Café), 28, 78, 82, 110, 129

Van Hill, 113, 115
Van Voorhies, 112
Veau qui tète, le (suckling calf), 6
Victor, General, 19
Vidrine, Chevalier de, 119
Vidrine, Josephine de, 119
Vidrine, Mademoiselle de, 120
Vigilant, Le (newspaper), 176
Vignié, Colonel Jean Baptiste Benjamin, 49, 152–155, 181
Villageois, Le (or The Villager) (newspaper), 124, 176
Villeré, Governor Jacques de, 38, 70, 74
Viole, Dr., 66
Viole, Mademoiselle, 66

Wartelle, Gabriel Pierre, 117, 126, 151, 188–189
Washington, George, 151, 169, 174
Washington, La., 117, 188
Wine and Olive Colony, see Société du Vin et de l'Olive

You, Dominique, 26, 29–30, 98, 131–132, 193